The Essential Vegan Travel Guide

2017 Edition

Caitlin Galer-Unti

ISBN 978-0-9986555-0-5

Caitlin Galer-Unti
The Vegan Word
Suite 74, 272 Kensington High Street
London W8 6ND
United Kingdom

Caitlin Galer-Unti
The Vegan Word
445 N. Park Blvd
Unit 5K
Glen Ellyn, IL 60137
USA

www.theveganword.com

Ordering Information:
Special discounts available for quantity purchases by corporations, charities, wholesalers, bookstores, educational institutions, others. For information please contact the publisher at the address above or by email: sales@theveganword.com.

Front Cover Photo: Santorini, Greece © Caitlin Galer-Unti
Cover Design by prodesignsx: https://www.fiverr.com/prodesignsx

Although the author and publisher have tried to provide as up-to-date of information as possible, they are not responsible for any injury, theft, loss, delays or melted dairy-free gelato.

For Lost Vegans Everywhere

Table of Contents

Introduction

Vegan Travel? Yes You Can!

• •

Picture it. You disembarked a 12-hour flight two hours ago, found your way to the train, and now you're clutching a white slip of paper as if it's going to save your life. You are bedraggled, you smell like you haven't showered all day (you haven't), you haven't slept in 27 hours (thank you, screaming baby on the plane), and you are starving because the airline forgot your vegan meal. All you've had to eat in the last 15 hours is a measly bag of airplane peanuts and an energy bar you managed to unearth from the depths of your bag (an amazing bit of contortion because you performed the dig to the bottom of your purse all the while strapped firmly into seat 28B, in between that smelly guy and the woman who kept elbowing you in the ribs every time she adjusted her seat).

The train arrives at its destination, but you are confused by the street signs (not surprising as you don't know the language). You clutch the white paper even harder, and approach people on the street and ask for directions. They don't understand you, so you point desperately at the address and the map, then gesture wildly (International sign language for: I'm lost). Eventually, your meaning seems to get through and the local resident points you down the street and to the right.

You smile (universal sign language for "thank you"), head down the indicated side street, where you are greeted with the most beautiful sight in the window of the restaurant. You've never been happier to see a trove of gleaming, fresh fruits and vegetables.. You practically sprint toward the display… But something feels wrong, a nagging feeling in the pit of your stomach (no, it's not hunger). Yep, it's definitely pitch black in that restaurant, and yes, they've pulled a grate down in front of the door.

What are you going to do? You've got the following options:

1. Wander back to that restaurant near the train station, the one with the aggressive waiter who shoved a menu at you as you walked past. Take a seat and communicate with international sign language that you want a plant-based meal. How would you even begin to do that? Wait and wait and wait for them to figure out your meaning and, then, serve you food. Eat whatever they bring you and hope for the best, pausing occasionally to pick off bits of bacon.

2. Meander up and down the nearby streets and see if you can find a grocery store that's open. Roam the aisles trying desperately to find a label written in English. End up buying a bunch of bananas and a tin of black beans. Eat, feeling depressed and deprived, and go to bed sort of full, but ultimately unsatisfied.

Fortunately, the above scenario is a thing of the past. No matter what anyone on the Internet says, vegan travelers do not need to starve, insult local cultures, or have to survive eating beans out of cans. You can travel and eat delicious, healthy meat-free food, in any country, and I'm going to show you how in this guidebook.*

*Disclaimer: I might not be able to help you out in Mongolia, which has one of the most meat-heavy diets in existence. Although who knows, because as of January 2017, Happycow.net has 20 listings for vegetarian, vegan and veg-friendly restaurants and stores in Mongolia.

Who's This Book For?

This book is for anyone who's ever been frustrated or worried about finding decent food on the road. Whether you're vegan, vegetarian or a healthy eater, don't worry, you can find food while traveling, and this book will show you how. We'll be focusing on finding vegan food, but you can easily adapt this advice to other dietary needs (e.g. vegetarian, gluten-free, etc.).

This book is also a great resource for expats who are moving abroad. You'll learn how to navigate a new and unfamiliar culture, make friends and find vegan food.

Their Objections – Your Solutions

"But you'll insult your hosts/host country by refusing to try their national dishes."
"But you'll never experience the real <insert country>. Everyone knows you can't really get to know a place unless you get to know their cuisine."
"What if you can't find any food? What if there aren't any vegetarian restaurants? What if you can't find any veggie options in other restaurants? What if you STARVE?"

All of these are actual sentences that you've probably heard when you've told people about your upcoming travel plans. I know, as I've heard them plenty of times. Some travelers have used these reasons as the basis for beginning to eat meat again.. Maybe you've even considered it. Perhaps you've previously had a bad food-related travel experience, and you found yourself wandering around a foreign city, admiring the street artwork, but absolutely fricking starving, unable to find anywhere offering decent food that fits with your diet and lifestyle. But let's unpack (verb use intentional as this is a travel guide) each of these arguments just a little bit.

"But you'll insult your hosts/host country by refusing to try their national dishes."

This is an irrelevant argument, because usually the people who utter this nonsense are exactly the sort of people you KNOW would never go to Mexico and try grasshopper tacos, or one of the various insect-inspired foods in Thailand. Also, I'm sure there are plenty of local traditions that even non-vegans might refuse to participate in – like bullfighting, child marriage or stoning gay people. Now, people may not understand why you don't eat animal products, especially in a culture without a history of vegetarianism, but the vast majority of people understand that different cultures have different traditions, and quite often you will find the "locals" are actually very interested in getting to know more about your culture and beliefs, including your diet. Even if you do run the risk of offending someone, somewhere, what is better – potentially risking offending a stranger, or going against your values and consuming a food that is the product of suffering and the cause of environmental destruction? If you regularly turn down these foods at home when friends and family offer them, why stop just because you're somewhere else?

"But you'll never experience the real <insert country>. Everyone knows you can't really get to know a place unless you get to know their cuisine."

A vast majority of people won't eat any and all local foods anyway. If someone asks you this, you can just retort, "Would you eat mealworms? Or cow testicles? Or an egg that's rotten and been buried for years?" (All local delicacies in some parts of the world!) Would they tell someone who's got celiac disease to avoid Italy because pasta is traditionally made with wheat flour (even though you can get a lot of gluten-free products in Italy these days)? I hope not! Besides, food is an important part of most cultures, sure, but is it the be all and end all? No! There's a lot more to experience of other cultures than just pastas, tapas or dim sum. There's also history, artwork, architecture and museums, to name but a few aspects of culture you'll experience in your travels. I should point out, too, that you can find vegan pastas, tapas, and dim sum.

"What if you can't find any food? What if there aren't any vegetarian restaurants? What if you can't find any veggie options in other restaurants? What if you STARVE?"

With a little bit of advance planning, this won't be an issue. And don't worry – over the course of this book, I'm going to show you exactly how to plan for success in adhering to your diet, from what websites and tools to use, to what to optimizing your search. This book is a complete DIY guide to researching and planning your trips, no matter where you're headed in the world. No matter where you go, you will always be able to arrive with a list of restaurants selected for your dietary needs. You'll learn how to make your own personal mini guidebook, if you will. And if you can't find any restaurants using the various tools outlined here, we'll go through other options. Like where to stay and what to eat in emergency situations. And even how to cook those canned beans in a coffeemaker in your hotel room.

Vegans Do It Better

Travel, that is. I'm going to put this out there: I enjoy travel even more as a vegan. Sure, maybe my restaurant choices are more limited, but that means I have to be choosier with where I eat. It means I can't just settle down at the first overpriced, tourist-trap restaurant I find. And I eat so much better for it.

Did I mention you're much less likely to have food poisoning as a vegan? (Just be careful about uncooked vegetables in countries where you're told to avoid the tap water.)

Oh, and you know what else? Vegan food tends to be lighter and healthier fare so you will feel less of that "oh God, I've overeaten and had so much fat and salt and feel so gross" vacation feeling.

Travel is all about discovery, feeling like you've found some never-before-seen corner of the world. It is a wonderful feeling when you've just discovered a vegan gem, or a fantastic vegan option hidden in a place you'd never have expected.

Travel is also all about connection. And you know what's a great way to feel connected to some stranger in a faraway place? Knowing you share a set of beliefs and a lifestyle. This far exceeds any benefit of "trying local cuisine." You'll get to try veganized versions of local cuisine and, if you're lucky, make new friends while you're at it. Vegans I've only just met have invited me to their homes, to stay with them, and to their birthday parties.

Finally, vegan restaurants are often in far-flung areas (the countercultural part of town, or a local university campus) so you will get away from the generic tourist areas and see a part of the city other tourists are unlikely to see.

Okay, But How Do I Do It?

By now you believe that not only is it possible to travel and find great healthy, plant-based food, but that it's actually a great experience and will allow you to explore aspects of a local culture you wouldn't see otherwise. But how do you actually go about it? Well, by using this little thing called the internet. Twenty-five years ago, you would have had to go to the library, or one of those places that sold books before we all downloaded them on the internet/Kindles. (Remember those things? They're called bookstores.) Then you would have to hope to find some sort of vegetarian guidebook on the place you were visiting. Or in the early days of the internet, maybe you'd have found someone on ICQ (an early internet chatroom) who was also vegan. Two of my friends met on ICQ. One owned such a guidebook on being vegetarian or vegan in Paris, a guidebook that wasn't in print where the other resided. So, the person with the guidebook, individually faxed every single page of said book to the other ICQ acquaintance. Which sounds like a pain. On the other hand, this guidebook faxing resulted in the creation of a lifelong, lasting friendship. My friends don't even live in the same country, but have visited each other every year since their ICQ exchange.

These days, the internet is brimming with information about every corner of the world, which you can use to your advantage, so long as you know how. Relax, sit back, and grab a soy latte or your favorite green tea, because in the coming pages I'll be showing you the tips and tricks I've acquired finding vegan food in the places I've traveled (30 countries and counting!).

Let's start off with some research methods (including some tricks I learned in my other career: researching niche blogs all over the world, from laundry blogs in Singapore to Nigerian Olympic sports blogs). Then we'll look at how to make connections with locals and make new friends, then work on how to put together a list of vegan-friendly restaurants. We'll look at how to choose where to stay, as well as an overview of the pros and cons of various types of accommodation and which are most vegan-friendly. I'll then prepare you for the trip, including how to eat on the plane and what to pack. We'll look at what to do when you get there, including tips for traveling with non-vegans and how to order at non-vegetarian restaurants, and what to do if you get stuck. Last, I'll give you a few recipes that you can make in a holiday rental kitchen or even a hotel room. Consider this book your vegan travel manual, a "how to" on surviving and thriving, wherever you end up in world, whether it's a quick weekend escape to a nearby city, a week-long vacation in Istanbul, or even a move abroad.

Before we start planning your trip, I need you to make a list of search terms we'll use throughout our research in Sections 1 and 2. I want you to make a list (on a piece of paper, like an old-fashioned person/hipster, or in Evernote, if you wanna be high-tech about it) of all the words you can think of related to your diet that might be helpful in searching for restaurants. Hang on to this, because you'll need it in the coming sections. Let me help you get started on your brainstorming:

Vegan
Vegetarian
Veg
Veggie
Plant-based
Healthy
Meat-free
Dairy-free
Etc.

Got your list? Okay, great! We're ready to go.

* * *

Notes

Section 1:

How the Hell Do I Find Somewhere to Eat?

Now that you've made your list of search terms, we're ready to start planning your trip. We're going to work under the assumption that you've already picked out a travel spot (if not, look for inspiration from the Top 10 Vegan Destinations of 2017 listed at the end of this book). Rather than choosing accommodations, we're going to focus on looking up vegetarian and vegan restaurants. Once you're familiar with where the restaurants are, then we'll move on to selecting a place to stay (Section 4).

We'll start by searching Google, before moving on to vegetarian restaurant directories such as HappyCow, local sites and blogs. Finally, we'll discuss how to make your own map and save it for offline use (in case you need to turn off your data while abroad).

Google Research

Why Google? Simply because it's the most widely used search engine. However, you can use the search engine of your choice. Just bear in mind that some of the tools and screenshots I show you in this section are Google-specific.

I'd suggest starting with a standard Google search, but you can also limit the timeframe if you just want recent results.

If you find a great site, you can use Google's "related" function, which finds sites similar to the URL you have entered. You just enter "related:" followed by the URL. So, for example, if you found veganlondon.co.uk and decided you liked it and wanted to find similar sites, you would type "related:veganlondon.co.uk" and it comes up with HappyCow London listings, an article in the Huffington Post on the top vegetarian restaurants in London, a Time Out feature on veggie eateries, etc. This is a very handy tool after you find a useful site or two!

Have a look around on Google, until you generate a list of websites. If you're going to a city with a large vegan or vegetarian population, you'll likely find a local vegetarian organization or even a website dedicated to vegan/vegetarian living in that city. This ultra-specific resource will be your new best friend, especially if it's carefully kept up to date! You'll likely also discover articles in local publications covering the best vegetarian/vegan restaurants in the area. Have a look at these rankings and see if there are any special restaurants you want to treat yourself to. You can also go onto Google maps, and search "vegan" or "vegetarian" – in big cities you will usually end up with a handy map of vegetarian restaurants. Here is an example:

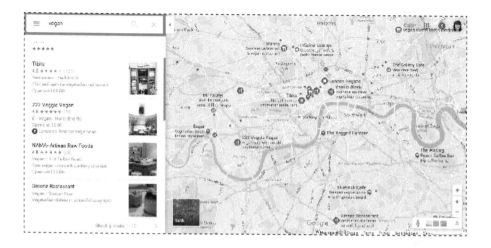

If you're going to a smaller city, or a city without a large vegetarian or vegan population, you might not find a dedicated vegetarian or vegan organization. But if it's an area frequented by visitors, you'll likely find some blog posts or articles about visiting the area as a vegan or vegetarian. You might have to dig a bit more than you would for, say, NYC, but you can come across some good resources for vegan Santorini. You'll just need to try out more search terms, and maybe go a few pages further into Google.

If you're not having much luck with your Google search, don't give up yet. There might not be many resources out there in English! Before you give up on Google, you should try the local version of Google. First, you'll need to find out what the Google address is for that country. For example, Google Spain is google.es, Google Brazil is google.com.br and Google Mexico is google.com.mx. It's usually some variation of either "google. com" or "google." followed by the country's two-letter ISO code. You can try guessing, or try Googling "Google Spain" or "Google Brazil". (Yes, I realize Googling Google is some sort of crazy meta-search.)

Once you're there on the local Google page, search in the local language (e.g. vegano in Spanish, végétalien in French). For example, type "Vegano Roma" into google.it. You can then further filter results into English results, Italian results, etc. Once on the individual webpage, you can auto-translate non-English sites into English (or the language of your choice) – if using Chrome, just right click and select "Translate to English."

If you're not getting many results from Google, don't worry. We're now going to delve into specific websites to use as tools. First up: HappyCow, everyone's favorite vegetarian restaurant directory!

Everyone's Favorite Site: HappyCow

Anytime you hear about vegetarian or vegan travel, you hear about HappyCow [http://happycow.net]. And with good reason. HappyCow is the most comprehensive directory of vegan, vegetarian, and vegetarian/vegan-friendly restaurants and stores around the world. HappyCow's always the place I start my searches. You can narrow down by continent, then country, and then city. You can even take advantage of the incredibly handy maps feature to viewall the restaurants in the city on a map.

Use the maps feature to decide where to stay and find a hotel near veggie restaurants (especially ones with good brunch options!). For some reason, vegan breakfasts and brunches can often be the hardest meal of the day to come by (with so many vegetarian restaurants only opening at lunchtime). So if you can assure yourself of having a breakfast (most important meal of the day, after all), then you've set yourself off to a good start.

Another useful feature is that if you've already booked somewhere to stay, you can enter the exact address of where you're staying (or the train station you arrive at, or any other address) and then see a map, along with the closest vegetarian restaurants.

This is useful in terms of seeing options around your hotel, but also for planning your days once you're there. If, for example, you're going to the modern art museum and know you'll want to eat lunch near the museum, you can search the location and see surrounding restaurants with veggie/vegan options.

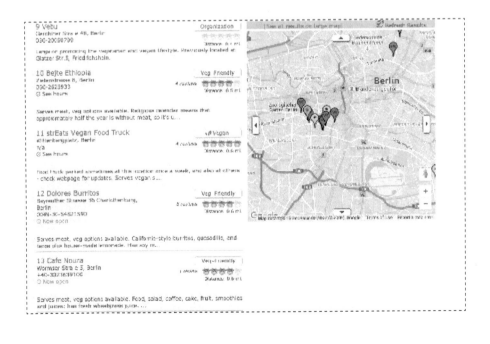

Bear in mind that HappyCow is a crowdsourced website, and its data is only as good as what its users enter on the site. So things might be out-of-date, particularly in less-visited cities. It's best to Google individual restaurants before you go (good to do anyway, in case they have temporarily closed while away on their summer vacation!). Better still, phone the establishment to check location and opening times. Remember that occasionally the information that comes up on Google can also be out of date, if no one has informed Google of a change of address or opening times. Here's what Google will show you when you search for a restaurant:

That's why it's best to phone the restaurant or find the restaurant's own website or Facebook page.

So to sum up, HappyCow's great, and if you've never used it, where have you been hiding? Under a lump of pink salt? But HappyCow's not the be-all and end-all – there are some other great sites out there which you should check out, as well as some iPhone/Android apps! These will make your life so much easier.

Other Directories

Apart from HappyCow, I've also had good results with VegGuide [https://www.vegguide.org]. While this may not be the best resource for planning a trip to Europe or Asia, it's great for researching restaurants in the US, and I've found that in many cities, it has even more listings than HappyCow. VegGuide seems to be better at listing non-vegetarian restaurants which have vegetarian and vegan options than HappyCow, which is superior at listing 100% veggie places. So, this might not be the best research tool if you're looking for a romantic all-vegan restaurant in Paris for a lover's getaway, but it's great if you're traveling to Akron, Ohio (19 listings on Veg Guide vs. HappyCow's 11) with your meat-eating grandma who's not that adventurous and doesn't really fancy trying a veggie restaurant.

There are also a plethora of apps you can download on your phone, with new ones seemingly springing up all the time. The best options are HappyCow (iOS/Android $3.99, international), Vegman (iOS, free, best for US), or Vegan Xpress (iOS, $1.99, listing of vegan options at chain restaurants across the US). These are fantastic if you have a smartphone, especially if you use the GPS for driving or walking, because most have map options where you can search for the nearest restaurants. When abroad, save cash by turning off your data and accessing the map features on the app over Wi-Fi. (In most places these days you only have to walk a few minutes to find the nearest café with free Wi-Fi!)

Local Sites

We touched on this briefly when we spoke about Google earlier – when you first Googled, you may have come across some local vegetarian or vegan sites. For example, a "vegan London" search yields this fantastic vegan London site, Vegan London [http://www.veganlondon.co.uk/], which covers all the bases in London, from vegan hotels to restaurants to activities and more.

When you come across a local site, see when it was last updated – active ones are usually more up to date than HappyCow because they're maintained by a local who is privy to all the new restaurant openings. If you're not able to find a local site, try searching for a vegan society/vegetarian charity for the country, and then see if they have local chapters. You may be able to find a local chapter's site – or contact – this way. For example, the North American Vegetarian Society (NAVS) maintains a list of local vegetarian chapters across North American cities. Even if they don't have restaurant listings, you can get in touch with the local chapter's contact. If you ask nicely, they're usually willing to help out a fellow veggie, and send you some suggestions of places to eat. Who knows, you might even make a new friend who wants to go for a coffee or show you around! Like I said, sharing the lifestyle with someone is usually a great starting point and connection, and one of the best parts of travel as a vegetarian or vegan is meeting with others!

Blogs

Alright, kids, it's story time! Sit down on the rug and listen up:

Once upon a time — *well, in South Korea around the year 2009, The Traveler (that's me!) was on her first trip to Asia. She'd been to Hong Kong, China, Taiwan, and now Korea, and while she'd loved all the yummy vegan food she'd eaten so far, she was getting desperate... for a muffin. Or a cookie. Or some sort of baked good. Any would do, really. It's just she hadn't had a sweet (or a savory, come to think of it) piece of floury goodness in her mouth in months. When some travelers get homesick, they go to McDonald's. Or Pizza Hut. Or an American bar. The Traveler really just needed to sit in a nice coffee shop, sipping a soy latte and eating a slice of vegan cake, as that was her true home. While searching Google, she stumbled across a blog called Alien's Day Out [http://aliensdayout.com/], which had the answers to all her problems.*

This magnificent blog spoke of a coffee shop that not only offered soy lattes, but pumpkin and squash lattes, along with vegan cakes baked by The Blogger herself! Without hesitation, The Traveler immediately got on the nearest train--she NEEDED that coffee. At the counter, The Traveler ordered the soy pumpkin latte and vegan cake that The Blogger had recommended in her blog posts. Then, something strange happened. A young woman seated at a nearby table stared at the intrepid traveler, and eventually called out, "You don't happen to be a reader of my blog, do you?"

The two women started talking, and made plans to meet up and go to a market. There The Blogger spoke in Korean (which The Traveler did not speak) to order delicious vegan delights. Afterward, The Blogger took The Traveler to a lantern festival, which The Traveler never would have found on her own. The Blogger also informed The Traveler that there was a new vegan restaurant located near hostel in which she was staying. The restaurant was so new that it had yet to appear on HappyCow and wasn't on any English vegetarian/vegan website.

Despite this restaurant being five minutes from her hostel, The Traveler would have left Seoul without ever having found it. That would have been a big shame because she had the most interesting food experience there, ordering what she thought was an ice cream sundae and ending up with shaved ice topped with beans. This is a traditional Korean dessert named patbingsu. The Traveler was so happy to have found the website and the café near her hostel, and was delighted to have a local friend who could show her around. And above all, she was elated to have found some vegan cake and coffee.

Lantern Festival
Seoul, Korea
2010

Blogs can be an excellent resource in your search for vegan places. There are two types of blogs you're likely to come across: bloggers based in the city you're visiting, and bloggers who've been there and reviewed it. Unfortunately, Google has discontinued its blog-only search, but you can still find blogs if you go deep enough in Google's search results, by including "blog" in your search (e.g. "Greece vegan blog"), or sometimes by limiting the date range you're searching (if you're not sure how, check Section 1). You can also limit your search by language. If you find blog posts about the city that are dated from a while ago, don't forget to check that the restaurants/stores mentioned are still open and in the same location!

Once you find bloggers who've visited (or are based in) the city, don't be afraid to email them directly, or leave a comment if you don't find their email address. (Tip: Their email is usually in the "About" or "Contact" section of the blog. Or try tweeting them. Most bloggers are regularly on Twitter and have Twitter buttons on their site which link to their Twitter profiles). Many bloggers love hearing from readers, and will be happy to help you with more information on the city. Again, if the blogger is based that location, they might even be willing to meet you for a coffee and some vegan cake! It would be nice if you treated them, though, as a "thank you" for the help they provided. Also, most bloggers love comments, so be sure to leave them a comment or send them a quick email or Tweet after your trip, letting them know you found their post(s) useful.

Looking for blogs? Check out this list of the Top Vegan Travel Blogs here (and while you're there, please vote for me, The Vegan Word, by clicking on the emojis!): http://bit.ly/vegantravelblogs

Barnivore

Now that you've found information on restaurants, a quick note about drinks. If you're like me and you mainly drink cocktails, then you can probably skip this section as most liquors are vegan (though not all - think of those worms in certain tequilas!). However, if you like beer and/or wine, Barnivore.com is an excellent resource for looking up which beers and wines (and liquors) are vegan. And liquors, too. It's easy to look on their database to see whether a given drink is vegan. However, you might want to download an app that uses the Barnivore database so that you can use it offline if you won't be able to use your data while on vacation. For this, I suggest iBarnivore (free, iOS), Vegaholic ($1.99, iOS), or VegeTipple ($1.99, Android).

Wait, you might be thinking. Alcohol isn't vegan?! That's right – some beers and wines are fined (the process that rids them of any sediment) using fish bladder or gelatin. But don't worry, because lots of beers, wines and other alcohols are fined in a completely vegan way (such as with clay or activated charcoal) and Barnivore makes it easy to find out!

Research Isn't Compulsory

That wraps up how to go about researching and finding vegetarian and vegan restaurants and drinks before your vacation. If you love planning your trips, poring over guidebooks and reading through Wikitravel guides, and deciding which sights to see, then you'll probably enjoy restaurant searching. If you're like me, and you refuse to read the Wikitravel guide until you're on the plane and loathe reading up on the destination beforehand, then you probably won't want to spend as much time reviewing restaurant listings. However, don't give up. Just try and think of it as an online adventure, a treasure hunt of sorts, where you're trying to find the buried treasure (somewhere in the vast pages of Google search results, there is one that actually tells you about vegetarian restaurants in that location!). But if you sit down at your computer and get all twitchy the minute you start thinking about exhaustively Googling and researching your destination, don't worry. The next section's for you.

* * *

Notes

Section 2:

Making Connections and Meeting New Friends.

• •

This section is all about how you can use the internet to find others who share your diet and lifestyle, and then use those connections to find plenty of food, as well as make new friends and have the trip of a lifetime. Because travel – and life – is almost always better when you make a connection. We're going to talk about how you can leverage the internet and your networks to find food recommendations – but also potential new friends in your destination.

Couchsurfing

Maybe you've heard of it. It sounds dangerous, and maybe a little gross. Staying on a stranger's sofa? "Yuck," you say. "Count me out!" Or maybe you're a super-adventurous type, and you think it sounds exciting. Imagine how much you could learn about their culture. Think of the stories! No matter what you think about Couchsurfing, you may not have thought of it as a way to meet other vegetarians and vegans. But that's exactly what it is – and it's also an opportunity to find out about the local plant-based food scene from people in the know, especially if Google leaves you in the lurch, with page after page of useless links.

Couchsurfing.org is a community project, which allows users (hosts) to offer up their sofas or spare rooms, and for other users who are visiting the area to request them. You register, put up some personal details, and then specify what you have available. You don't have to have a sofa or space to host someone in your house. You can just offer to meet people for coffee. It's a great tool to meet travelers in your town, and engage in cultural exchange, and it's also a fantastic tool for when you're traveling, even if the thought of staying on some random person's sofa gives you goosebumps. Couchsurfing is not just for crashing on people's sofas, ladies and gents! It's about meeting people, learning about different cultures and – yes, really – it can also be about finding other vegans. So to find them, we need to do an advanced search. Again, you'll need your keyword list handy. We'll be searching people's profiles for those words!

First, if you don't have an account, you'll need to set one up. It's free to register, and free to sleep on these strangers' sofas (although it's nice to bring them a little gift if you can)! Once you've got an account set up, you'll need to search by filtering the city you're looking for. You can further select by types of "couch" available and male or female host, but at this point just filter by city – we're just looking for people to make friends with, rather than find a place to sleep! (If you want to use Couchsurfing to find a place to stay, we'll cover that in Section 4.)

The most important bit for our purposes is in the advanced search options: we want to do a keyword search, using our keywords from our original list like vegan, vegetarian etc. You'll find people who have mentioned these words in their profiles. IMPORTANT: it's really critical to read each individual profile! What we're doing here is just a keyword search to find mentions of the words, which does NOT mean that the person is a vegan or vegetarian or into healthy eating. Sometimes you will find that they've actually said something like "I'm a dedicated carnivore who hates meatless food with a passion." And they've turned up in your search for the word "meatless." That's why it's really important to read their profile – you don't want to be messaging them asking for tips on the best vegetarian restaurants!

Let's say you've found a few people who mention your keywords in their profile and you've read their profiles to check they are actually veggie or interested in vegetarian or vegan food... Now the fun bit starts! If you haven't set up your own profile, you should do so now, before you contact anyone. If your profile is blank, people will be less likely to respond. Couchsurfing may consist of meeting relative strangers or letting them stay with you, but people still want to know a bit about you first! Send a message to the people you've found and tell them you're interested in meeting them for coffee, and learning more about where to find healthy/meat-free/vegan options in the city. Mention something about their profile to show you've actually read it and are not just spamming them with a message. It helps if you make a personal connection, especially if you find a common interest in addition to diet and lifestyle (like you both really love heavy metal, or you're both into skateboarding).

Couchsurfing has bailed me out of trouble many a time, so I strongly advise you to use it if you run into any difficult situations as well, for example if you aren't able to find any vegetarian restaurants or places with veg options. If you can find someone on Couchsurfing, they can probably help you out!

Here are a few of the many ways Couchsurfing has saved me:

Croatia, 2009

I did my homework and my planning and found the one vegetarian restaurant in Dubrovnik at the time (which I subsequently ended up visiting every single day of the week I was there, and sampling everything vegan on the menu, as well as making good friends with the owner, who gave me a lot of free muffins). However, my plane landed on a Sunday evening, the one day the restaurant was closed. I knew I'd be too tired to want to wander around trying to find a supermarket (and the B&B I was staying in didn't have a kitchen). I messaged a vegan on Couchsurfing who immediately told me where I could get a cheeseless pizza. I was so glad I'd sent that message, because when I landed I discovered 95% of restaurants were seafood restaurants and if I hadn't had the address of the pizza place I might have gone withou dinner, or had to make do with a dinner of beans from a can.

Argentina, 2010

I was nearly stranded without a place to stay over Christmas. Everywhere I turned was booked up, even though I was in the huge metropolis of Buenos Aires. I couldn't find a single hostel or decently priced hotel — the only things that seemed to be available were ridiculously overpriced. In an act of desperation, I messaged a seemingly friendly vegetarian girl asking to stay the next day. And she said yes! I ended up in a really amazing flat with my own en-suite bathroom, and we had a lot of fun cooking a vegan dinner together and discussing veganism, as she was interested in going vegan.

Chile, 2010

I didn't know a soul in Santiago and, after a couple of months of traveling, was starting to get lonely. I messaged a vegan who not only took me out for a fun night on the town, but also gave me a long list of suggested vegan restaurants and even a store to visit.

Santa Lucia Park
Santiago, Chile
2010

Meetup

If you haven't checked out Meetup.com yet, do so now. It's an amazing resource for finding like-minded individuals in your area, and joining activities geared toward your area of interest! Simply search your city, and interest areas (like blogging, veganism, knitting and more). It's also a fantastic place to find people with shared interests in the city you're visiting. You could use it to find people who share your love of softball and who want to go for a game, but in our case we're going to use it to find fellow plant eaters.

You can set a city and the number of miles to include in your search radius, so set it to something like "within 10 miles of XXX [city you will be visiting]". Next, enter your search terms – pick one of the words from your keyword list. If there's a vegetarian Meetup group in that city, then great – sign up! It's free to create an account on Meetup.com, and join different groups.

You'll likely need to provide a little information about yourself, like why you want to join the group. Sometimes you are able to join a group with the click of a button and sometimes the administrator of the group needs to approve your application. This will usually only take a day or so.

Once you've signed up and joined the group or been approved, have a look and see if they're planning a Meetup (like visiting a veggie restaurant, having a picnic, or another activity) while you're in the area! You'll need to RSVP so that the organizers know you're attending. In the case of smaller venues, they may have a limit on the number of people who can attend. If you are put on the Waitlist because all the spots at the venue are taken, keep checking back because if anyone changes their RSVP from "yes" to "no" the people on the Waitlist will be given a spot at the Meetup.

Meetups are free to attend unless otherwise noted on the Meetup page, but if it's a meal or drinks, you'll be expected to pay your part of the tab, of course. If they're not holding an official group event, but you want to meet people, you can post in the members' area of the group and see if anyone is up for meeting unofficially. Or you can suggest an event to the organizer. (Depending on the group settings, there is sometimes an option to suggest an event.) Or if you're struggling to figure out where you should go in the city, you can write a message in the forum/members' area asking for suggestions!

And like I said, it's all about making a connection. And most people are really keen to help out a fellow vegan/vegetarian. When I was visiting Beijing, I signed up to the Beijing vegan meet up and RSVP'd to attend one of the dinners – which just happened to be the week I was there! Lucky! Unfortunately, I got a horrible flu and was bedridden much of the week in the hostel. It was pretty miserable for a couple of days, until I sent the Meetup organizer a message saying I wouldn't be able to attend the dinner as I was so ill. She replied right away, saying how sorry she was that I was sick, and recommending a Chinese herbal tea that I could get in any drugstore. Armed with her recommendation, I went to the drugstore around the corner the very next morning, and felt better after my very first cup. Unfortunately I didn't improve in time for the Meetup, but the tea saved my trip. I nearly ended up missing the Forbidden City due to my illness, but recovered just in time to get out of the hostel and see the sights!

Forums

Forums are another great resource for finding out about restaurants and for connecting with locals. Check out the forums on The Post Punk Kitchen [http://forum.theppk.com/] and The Vegan Forum [http://www.veganforum.org/]. *Note: in late 2016 PPK announced the forums were closing but as of January 2017 they are still up.

If you haven't been on a forum before, it's normally arranged into boards. If the forum were a neighborhood, the boards would be the houses. Each board has a theme. For example, you might have Europe, North America and Australia as boards. Then within each board, you have a thread. This is like a room in a house, and it's where you'll find all the people at the forum-party. These are the topics. You can start a new thread, or respond to an old one. It's considered polite to have a search through the archives before starting a thread, to make sure one doesn't already exist. Hey, if you were throwing a party, and someone was already hosting one in another room in the same house, it would be a bit rude to start an entirely new party! If you search and you do come across a thread, but it's a couple of years old, feel free to bring it back to life by commenting on the thread. Don't worry, even though it's old, people will still see it. Your comment will "bump" the thread – that means it will become visible again at the top of the board, and everyone accessing the board will see it as soon as they click on the board. If you search and don't come across anything, start your own new thread. You can post where you're going and see if anyone else has been there on vacation and has recommendations, and you can also try and connect with local veggies. Who knows, a group of locals might even be hosting a meet soon in the city you're visiting, or they might be willing to meet up with you!

Social Networks

Maybe someone you are connected with on Facebook or Twitter or Instagram has been to (or is from!) the place you're visiting, and you don't even realize it. Or perhaps they know someone who has. It's always worth posting on Facebook or Twitter that you're going there, and asking whether anyone has any recommendations. Even if they don't, they might be able to put you in touch with someone who does. A Facebook friend who I don't know very well recently posted she is going to Berlin and Austria, and was inundated with suggestions of what to do and where to eat. I don't speak to her very frequently (the last time we spoke was probably a year ago), but it came up in my feed so I added a few suggestions too.

On Facebook, there's an extremely helpful group called Vegan Travel (just search for it and request to join) where you can post all your vegan travel questions. There are thousands of members so it is likely that someone in the group has been to the place you are visiting and can help you out!

On Twitter, try adding hashtags to your tweet so people can find you more easily. For example, #vegantravel, or you can be more specific like #veganberlin. Before posting, try checking on the search tool to see if anyone else has been tweeting with that hashtag recently. It will give you an idea of how popular and active the hashtag is. You might also find some useful tweets about the city that people have sent using that hashtag!

Asking People

Good old-fashioned offline conversations are another great way to make connections and find out about places to go. Reach out to vegetarians and vegans you know in your hometown. (If you don't know any, try looking at Meetup and Couchsurfing to see if there are any local groups with which to connect!) See if anyone has been to the place you're visiting, and ask for recommendations. Likewise, see if your friends have any contacts who live there. They might be able to put you in touch with locals, who are more likely to want to advise you and meet up with you if you're a friend of a friend. Don't you find that a mutual connection can serve as a "reference" and that you're more likely to want to help out someone connected to you, however distantly? As humans, we're wired to behave like this. With so much sensory information coming in, we implicitly trust our connections, and by extension, their connections.

You can also try to get some recommendations through word of mouth once you've actually arrived at your destination. Just go to the vegan restaurants and health food stores you've discovered through your online research and ask them for suggestions of other places to go. These proprietors might be able to tell you about new places, which aren't even listed online yet. Thanks to their local connections and – you guessed it – good old-fashioned word of mouth, you'll find recently opened restaurants!

* * *

Section 3:

Organizing Your Trip.

• •

Okay, so you've made your list. You've exhausted the internet, and asked every great-aunt and friend-of-a-friend you can think of if they've been to your destination. You've searched every word you can think of, you've looked at Google search results to approximately page 5823. You've asked for advice on every forum and social network you're a member of (you even joined some new ones!). You've got a nice fat list of restaurants to visit. But now what do you do? How do you keep track of everything?

Make a Folder or Booklet

My suggestion is to make yourself a booklet or folder with the most important information. You can simply print it all off as separate web pages from HappyCow/Meetup/etc., and put it in a big folder to take with you, alongside your plane tickets and hotel reservations. If you want to save particular articles, you can print those off – or, my favorite option, save them to an app (like Evernote or Pocket) for offline use. At the end of this book you'll find a list of my favorite apps to download. Evernote is a notebook app, which allows you to create docs, save pieces of text and quotes, and keep them super organized into different folders. I'm not into filing systems, but people I know who love filing and organizing are absolutely in love with their Evernote. One downside is you can no longer view them offline unless you upgrade to a (paid) premium account. My preferred app is Pocket, which allows you to save whole web pages to view offline – for free. You can also use Pinterest to create a visual board for your trip and Pin webpages that you find and want to save – for example restaurants, hotels, and attractions.

Key information I'd suggest including:

- Each restaurant, with name, address, opening times, phone number and email.

- Translations of key words and phrases.

- List of traditional local foods that are likely vegan.

- Map with your hotel and some nearby veg restaurants marked on it.

Putting Your Information Together: Google Maps

Okay, so now you have all your information together for your folder or booklet, including your list of restaurants, translations of local phrases, and local "accidentally vegan" dishes. But what if you don't want to waste paper and ink? What about going digital? I'd definitely recommend creating your own Google map if you're traveling within your country and can use the internet on your phone without being charged exorbitant fees, or if money is no object and you don't mind using your phone abroad, or if you're going to get a local SIM card that allows you to use data at a decent price. (This is great if you're going to be somewhere for a bit longer term.) If you're anything like me, you basically can't find your way around without your map on your phone and your GPS. You probably follow that little blue dot mindlessly around, not even stopping to look up – if it tried to walk you straight through a solid building, you probably would!

But what if you're going to be abroad and unable to use the search function on maps? You can save the map for offline use – and even "star" restaurants, attractions, and other places of interest for offline use. Your phone will let you use the map (including the lifesaving little blue dot which shows you where you are!) even when you aren't connected to the internet. This is the most amazing thing ever when you're abroad and you've had to turn off your data. It means that suddenly, you can have a map that shows you where you are at any time. No more getting lost in strange cities! Unfortunately it can't give directions or use the phone's compass function unless you're connected to the internet.

While you can't search for directions on the go without an internet connection, you can connect your phone to the internet, search for directions, go offline, and then follow those directions, as long as you don't restart your phone at any point while you are en route. So try entering your destination while connected to your hotel internet, or on free Wi-Fi found in a café, and then going offline and following said map.

To save a map for offline use on your phone, pull up a map of the city. Zoom out until you have as much of the city (and surrounding areas) on your screen as possible. Google will only save the area shown on the screen for offline, so make sure to get in as much as possible. However, bear in mind it can only save 50km by 50km at a time, so if the map you want to save is too big you may want to do a few saves, zooming in on different parts of the map. Oh, and if Google gives you an error ('cannot save') it's probably because you're zoomed too far out (like trying to save an entire country!) and it's too much information for Google to handle. Zoom in a little, and try again. Depending on how big the city is, you might be able to save the entire city in one go, or you might need to save different areas of the city at a time, depending on where you're planning to go and how much of the map you need.

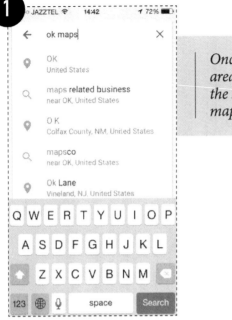

Once you've got the right area on your screen, click on the search bar and type "ok maps".

It will come up with the following screen after you hit "enter".

Click "download" and it will prompt you to give the map a name.

4

Once you've named the map and clicked "save" you will get a screen telling you the map is saving.

5

To star a place, drop a pin where you want to go. (To drop a pin, simply hold your finger on the location for a few seconds, and a pin will drop), then click "favorites" and it will be starred. Or, look up a restaurant, hotel, or attraction and once this screen comes up, click on the name of the restaurant:

6

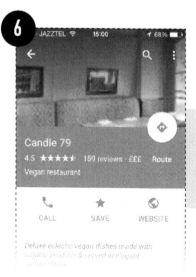

On the next screen, click on the star button:

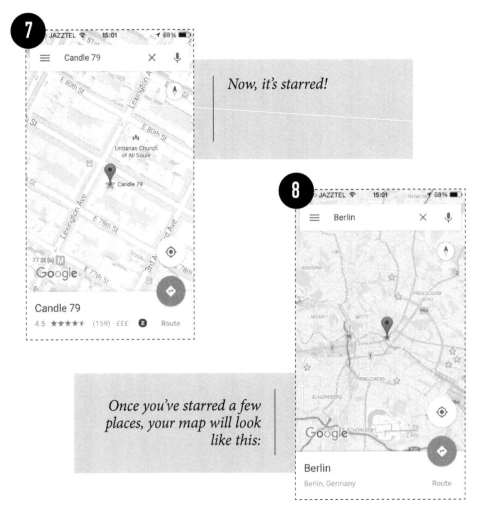

Now, it's starred!

Once you've starred a few places, your map will look like this:

You can see the stars on our map later, even when you're offline. Sadly, you won't be able to search for individual places or restaurants and directions when you're offline, so it's important to save the map and star any special places before you're cut off from Wi-Fi! You can do this before your trip, or if you have Wi-Fi in your hotel/hostel/apartment, save it in the morning before you go out for the day.

Or you could go the really old-fashioned route, and print out some paper maps, just like in the anecdote in this guidebook's introduction. Just make sure you've double checked the restaurants' opening hours (unlike in the story)! I find the easiest way to do this is to print out some maps showing each restaurant/store you want visit. Ideally, the map you make should be zoomed in a bit on the local area so you can see the nearest streets. Then, once you reach your destination, get one of those paper fold-out maps of the city they give away free at most hostels, hotels and airports. Take a pen, and using the paper maps you printed out before, locate each restaurant on the map and mark it in pen, with the name. That way, when you're wandering around looking at the sights, you'll be able to look at your map, spot your location on the map, and see which restaurants are nearest.

A final note: Carefully plan for your first meal upon arrival– you may be really hungry and tired when you get off the plane. I suggest using HappyCow/Google maps to find the restaurant closest to your apartment/hotel/hostel/Couchsurfing host, check that they'll be open upon your arrival, and make and print a Google map with directions from your lodging to that restaurant. That way, when your plane lands, you can go check into your hotel, take a quick shower (if needed), and go straight to that restaurant when it's time for lunch/dinner. If you don't find anything within walking distance, find the location of the nearest metro station, and locate a restaurant that's easy to get to via metro. Trust me, when you first arrive and are jetlagged, the last thing you want to be doing is wandering around, trying to find a restaurant that's open, not really sure where you're going or if you're in a safe area.

Likewise, plan your last meal – if your flight leaves at an awkward time, you might want to stock up on food prior to your departure. You want to have some goodies to take with you on the plane and to tide you over before and during your flight (and, you never know when an airline will forget your vegan meal).

Looking up Opening Times and Addresses

Want a sure way to go hungry and get in a massive fight with your travel companions? No? Well then you better double-check the location and hours of the restaurants on your list. Don't just trust HappyCow, or even Google. I know from personal experience what can happen if you don't check opening times!

It was our very first holiday together as a couple.

We'd only been together a few months, and this was a huge test of our relationship. I know that travel can bring out the best and worst in a person, and so we knew going into it that this would be one of our first – and most important – tests as a couple. It would make or break us. Imagine my dismay when, after getting off the flight and getting the bus into town, we found ourselves, stomachs growling, wandering through the sunbaked streets of Bratislava, Slovakia in search of a vegan restaurant that was not at the listed street address.. Eventually, over an hour into our wanderings, we decided we had to stop and call the restaurant, and upon going to their website to search for the number, discovered that the restaurant was not where HappyCow or Google said it would be. The restaurant had moved! HappyCow, which relies on its users for reviews and updates, had not yet been informed of the move Nor had Google updated the new location on Maps or on their search page results. Fortunately, we were able to get to a nearby vegan-friendly restaurant (found on the list I had created prior to departure) and get there before our rumbling stomachs caused a fight – and ruined our weekend.

So, how can you prevent stress, arguments with your traveling companions and dehydration brought on by walking around in the baking hot sun searching for a restaurant that may have moved? Start with your list of restaurants and stores, and look up, at minimum, the opening days and hours (noting down in particular any days each restaurant is shut, or days it closes early) and the address. If you think you may want to call them once there, write down the phone numbers, too. You can even email in advance and verify the times they're open, and the days you're going. It's also a good idea to make sure things aren't closed because of holidays, especially if you're going over traditional holidays (Christmas, New Year's, Chinese New Year, etc.) or times when a lot of the local population is away and restaurants may be temporarily closed. Be prepared to be surprised by local holidays you didn't even know existed.

For example, one year during our summer holidays in Sicily, we discovered that everyone else in Sicily was on holiday, too. Pretty much the whole island (like much of Italy) was closed for the month of August. Just about everyone had headed off on their own holiday, making Palermo a ghost town. Restaurant after restaurant I'd eagerly anticipated visiting was shuttered. Luckily, we didn't starve – but I did learn an important lesson: to check local holidays!

Look up any traditional holidays occurring during the time you're visiting, or check individual restaurants' sites, Twitter, or Facebook. (Twitter and Facebook are often the best places to check because they are updated frequently and many restaurant owners post when they're about to close for holidays.) Not all restaurants do post notices, though, so don't assume they will do so. (If in doubt, or you know a local holiday is coming up, always email or call.)

If you've created a folder or Evernote file, note restaurant opening times and up-to-date addresses.

Don't Starve Just Because It's Sunday

Okay, so now you should have a list of restaurants, and also their opening times (and addresses). Have you started to notice any trends in days when restaurants are closed? In many places, there's a day when most restaurants are closed. It's commonly Sunday or Monday. If you're in a place where there's a day like this, you might find it hard to eat on that day, so it's important to note which restaurants are open that day. You can check your list by going through each restaurant individually, or you can use an app. Doodle isn't made for this purpose at all, but it fits the bill. If you're not familiar with Doodle, it's a really cool free scheduling app, which helps you pick a time for a group of people to meet based on everyone's availability. You enter some details about the event plus days and times, and people go in and write down their names and whether or not they can attend at those times – and Doodle tells you which day is most popular. Handy if your friends, like mine, are so busy you can't even find a day to go for a drink together! We're going to use Doodle to visually see when restaurants are open. It will look like this, with green ticks representing the restaurant being open, and red "Xs" that it's closed.

To make a Doodle, you simply start by choosing dates from a calendar. In our example, we'll assume you are visiting Barcelona for the weekend, from late morning Friday until Sunday afternoon.

Doodle

5 participants	October 2017 Fri 13		Sat 14			Sun 15
	Friday Lunch	Friday Dinner	Saturday Breakfast	Saturday Lunch	Saturday Dinner	Sunday Breakfast
Sesamo		✓			✓	
Teresa Carles	✓	✓	✓	✓	✓	✓
Rasoterra	✓	✓		✓	✓	
Cat Bar		✓			✓	
Dolce Pizza y los Ve	✓	✓		✓	✓	
Your name	☐	☐	☐	☐	☐	☐

Go to Doodle's homepage [http://doodle.com] and click on "schedule event." It will ask you to fill out the name of the event and your email address (don't worry, Doodle won't spam you):

Doodle

Schedule an event

1. **General** ▸ 2. Time proposals ▸ 3. Settings

Title

Barcelona Weekend

Location (optional)

Description (optional)

Your name

Next, Doodle will ask you to choose the dates – in this example, we'll choose the days you will be in Barcelona:

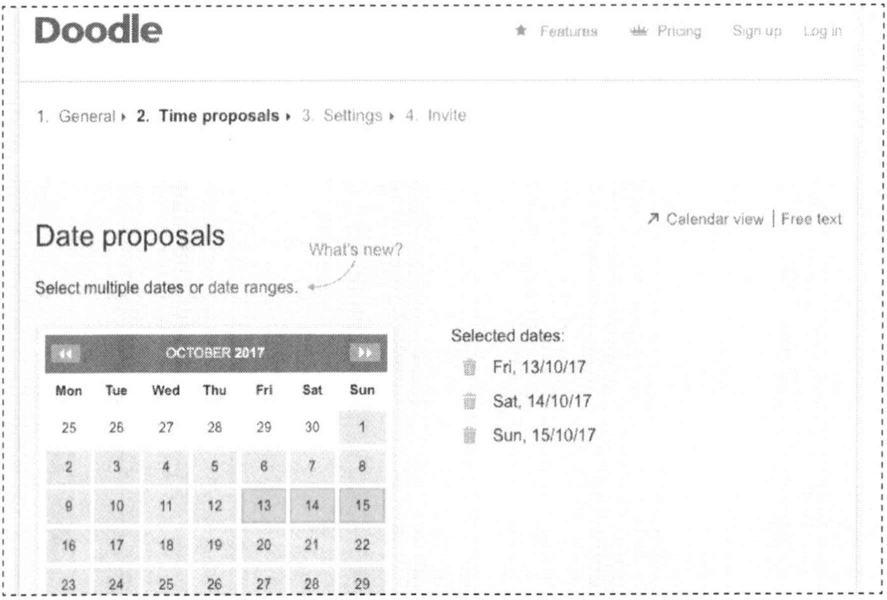

The next screen will ask you to choose times. I'd suggest choosing mealtimes for each day:

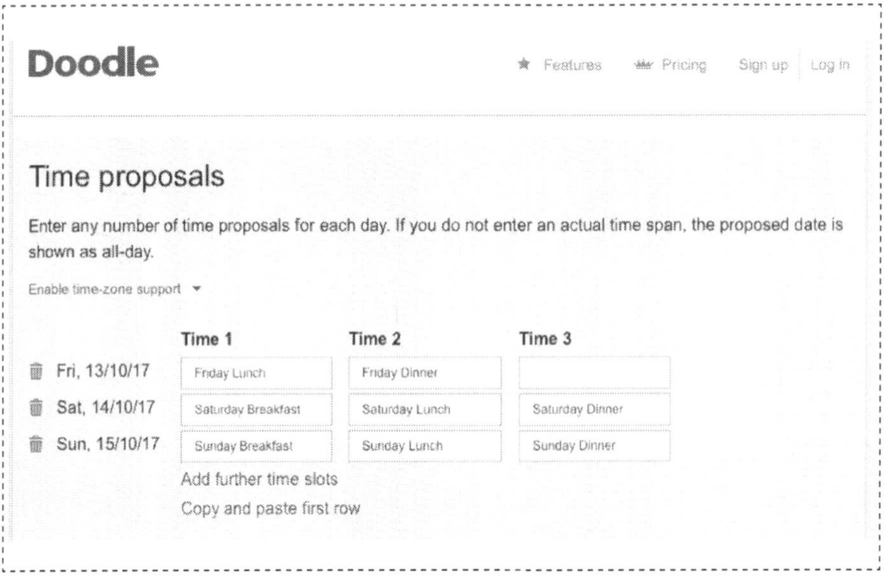

After this, you can select the basic poll option:

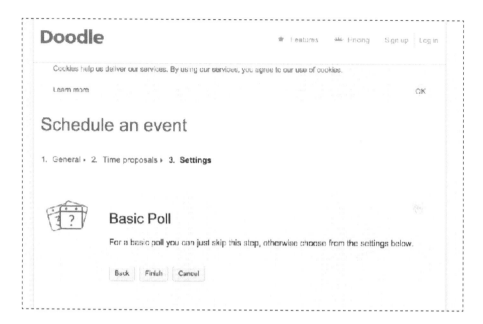

After you select the basic poll option, you'll receive a "participation link" to the poll on the next screen (and in your e-mail). Go to the participation link, and you'll be given the option to put your name in and participate in the poll. Here, you'll put the name of each restaurant and tick each time of day that they're open. For example, Sesamo in Barcelona is open from 8pm to midnight every day except Monday, so we will put Sesamo and tick "Friday dinner" and "Saturday dinner," then click the "save" button:

We'll need to go back to the poll and complete for each restaurant on our list. We'll end up with the poll results from the first screenshot:

	October 2017 Fri 13		Sat 14			Sun 15
5 participants	Friday Lunch	Friday Dinner	Saturday Breakfast	Saturday Lunch	Saturday Dinner	Sunday Breakfast
Sesamo		✓			✓	
Teresa Carles	✓	✓	✓	✓	✓	✓
Rasoterra	✓	✓		✓	✓	
Cat Bar		✓			✓	
Dolce Pizza y los Ve	✓	✓		✓	✓	
Your name	☐	☐	☐	☐	☐	☐

For example, this shows me that if we're looking for a place for breakfast Sunday, we should choose Teresa Carles, as all the other restaurants are closed for breakfast.

Translations

Okay, you're thinking, that's all well and good, but what am I supposed to do if I search, and search, and search and can't find any vegan restaurants? What if I've exhausted all the resources, and I still can't find anything? Well first of all, you might want to consider a self-catered option. If you've got your own kitchen, you have a great deal more flexibility, and you won't need to worry about whether or not you can find restaurants that cater to your dietary needs. However, you probably still want to be able to eat out. You're on holiday, after all, so you don't want to be slaving away in the kitchen all day!

This is where the internet comes in handy yet again. (We should all say a massive thank you to the internet for its existence now, and for making our lives so much easier in so many ways!) Now, instead of asking the internet about vegetarian or vegan restaurants in your destination, we'll be looking up how to say vegetarian/vegan (and a few other words) in the local language, along with researching local traditional foods which you can eat.

Did you know that there's a special magic word in Thai ("jay") that you can say that will pretty much guarantee you vegan food in any restaurant? Or that this word ("jay") and a similar word ("chay") can be used in Laos ("jay"), Vietnam ("chay"), and Cambodia ("chay")?

Thanks to the internet, we can find out about local traditions and words in other languages without ever leaving our sofa or meeting someone from that country.

First things first, you may want to consider getting a Vegan Passport. These are little books produced by the Vegan Society and made to fit easily in a handbag or backpack, which you're meant to hand to your server in a restaurant. The book explains, in 85 languages, that you're vegan, and what you do and don't eat. You can easily pick one up online or at vegan festivals, or you can download the app for iOS or Android for $1.99.

If you are planning on shopping in supermarkets or health food stores and want to be able to scour ingredients lists you have the option of buying the European Vegan Zine. This booklet contains translations of common animal ingredients and additives, so you can easily check ingredients lists in any European language.

If you don't want to buy a Vegan Passport, or you have other dietary requirements, you can make your own list of translations in the local language and bring these with you (or put them in your folder or booklet).

My free gift to you as a thank you for purchasing this book is a handy wallet-sized card of phrases to translate which you can print, cut out and put into your wallet. You can download yours here: https://theveganword. com/evtg-gift/

Where should you get your translations? Well, Google Translate does a fairly decent job with simple words and phrases, but the more complicated your phrases get, the more Google Translate may struggle. Of course, you won't know whether the translation is perfect or not until you try it. So you should probably check your translations against a few sites, and if you know anyone who speaks the language, ask them for help! If you found any new contacts via Couchsurfing, you can also ask them, or post some questions on your Twitter, Facebook or other social networks and see if any of your friends or their friends speak the language and can help out. You never know who might be following you and what languages they speak!

Eating Like a Local

It's also worth having a look at local traditions, and finding out if there are any holidays or religious traditions that encourage veganism or vegetarianism. Normally, you'll find that these celebrations are religious. Examples of such holidays are Eastern Orthodox Lent (for which many followers go vegetarian) or the Buddhist Vegetarian Festival in Thailand. Read up on the local religions and any festivals or holidays, and discover whether any of them involve vegetarianism.

Did you know, for example, that in Ethiopia there's a time of year and certain days of the week when you can expect a large portion of the population to be eating vegan, and therefore vegan food is a lot easier to come by? (Those times are Lent, Wednesdays and Fridays.)

Or that in Romania and Russia a large portion of the population eats mainly vegan during Lent and prior to Christmas?

Finally, read and learn about local foods and find out whether any traditional dishes look like they're accidentally vegan or vegetarian (or easy to modify). For example, quite often in Italy marinara pizza is available which is simply a pizza with tomato sauce and garlic with no cheese. (This is a very traditional, very basic pizza marinara.) In Greece, there are lots of accidentally vegan dishes, like the hummus-like "fava," which is a bean purée made from yellow split peas. You might just discover a new favorite dish to recreate when you get home!

The best way to find these sorts of "accidentally vegan" dishes is to go back to your list of words on Google, but expand your search to encompass an entire region or country instead of the city, and maybe add on "dishes" or "foods" into your search, for example:

- Vegan Greek dishes
- Vegetarian traditional Italian foods

* * *

Section 4:

Where to Stay & How to Choose.

Now that you've created your list of restaurants, your translations of phrases, and information on local foods that are usually vegan, you're ready to choose where to stay! In this section, we'll be discussing how to use your list of restaurants to pick the most vegan-friendly area to stay. Then, we'll discuss the pros and cons of different accommodation options, including hotels, B&Bs and guesthouses, hostels, Couchsurfing, Airbnb, housesitting, Vegvisits, and renting a holiday apartment.

Find a Vegan-Friendly Area

When choosing a place to stay on holiday, people typically run through a laundry list of their own personal priorities. Your priorities might include cost, location, proximity to the airport or public transit, cleanliness, Wi-Fi service, recreational facilities (e.g., a pool), atmosphere, noisiness and safety. You may also want to consider the vegetarian- and vegan-friendliness of the lodging. If breakfast is served, do they have a vegan option? Is there a refrigerator in the room? If it's a hostel, does it have a kitchen so you can cook? Is it close to vegetarian restaurants? We're going to talk about a variety of different options of accommodation options, as well as what questions you should be asking. Before we do that, though, I just want to discuss, in really general terms, the selection of a location/neighborhood. Now, putting all other considerations aside (hey, keep your list of priorities, just put your notebook down for a second), we're going to think just about how to choose a vegan-friendly location.

Have a look on HappyCow (using the map feature, go to the city you're going to and then pull up the map of the city) and it will look something like this:

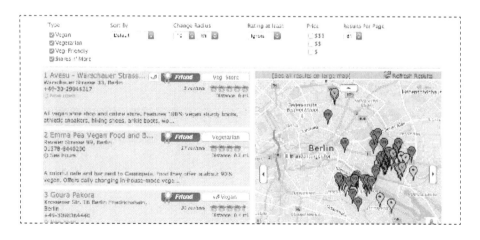

Identify the greatest concentration of vegetarian restaurants (hint: normally in the city center, surrounding a university, or in an area known for counterculture), and then look for places to stay in that vicinity. Alternatively, you might want to consider places which are close to a restaurant with vegan breakfast/brunch options, or places near a restaurant that you want to go to for dinner, or near a health food store if you're renting a place with kitchen facilities. Or, if you're like one of my friends, look for a place that has a freezer and is near a store selling vegan ice cream (#priorities)!

Once you've located a neighborhood in which you want to stay, you now have a plethora of lodging choices: hotel, hostel, Airbnb, Couchsurfing, B&B, apartment rental, canoe (okay, maybe not the last one… although you can stay in a boat hostel in Stockholm). We're going to examine each accommodation type in terms of pros and cons (with relation to vegetarian-friendliness) as well as consider which options are best (depending on your situation and city) and the types of questions you should ask prior to renting.

Hotels

This might be (or at least it used to be) the standard option for many travelers, but it's my least favorite. Not just because hotel chains tend to be standardized and lacking character, but because they don't afford many options for us. They usually don't have kitchens or many times are devoid of fridges (unless you upgrade to a suite), and if they offer one of those standard hotel breakfast buffets, they probably won't many vegan options laid out. If you're going to book a hotel, make sure you have some vegan breakfast options in the local vicinity, have checked with the hotel to determine whether or not they will be able to accommodate you at breakfast, or have a plan for what you can eat in the room. For example, bring some quick-cook oatmeal and make it with the tea kettle/coffeemaker in your room, or have fruit for breakfast. For recipes to make in a coffeemaker, check Section 7. Alternatively, buy cereal and some single-serving sized UHT soymilk cartons – that's the kind of container that you can leave out of the fridge. Some hotels are getting better at stocking soy milk, or will be willing to get some in if you ask in advance, so you might be able to have coffee and cereal.

You can look for apartment hotels, which are hotels consisting of mini apartments with small kitchens, and can be an inexpensive option in some cities.

On the plus side, if you stay in a really posh, five-star hotel, they will almost certainly cater to your needs and even if their restaurant doesn't have any vegan options on the menu, they will very likely make something for you on request.

My favorite place to book a hotel is Hotels.com, because they offer an excellent reward system – for every ten nights you book through their website, you get one night free! If you're traveling last minute, though, you might want to try Lastminute.com or Hotel Tonight (a free app).

B&Bs and Guesthouses

B&Bs can be a really great option, if you find one that's willing to make you a vegetarian or vegan breakfast. You can even find some vegetarian and vegan B&Bs, which are excellent, because not only will you be fed a morning meal without having to worry about it, you can probably even get tips from the B&B owner about nearby restaurants with vegetarian and vegan dishes! Some guesthouses serve breakfast and also have the option of buying dinner, which makes your life even easier, because you can always go back to the guesthouse if you can't find any vegan options. This option works great in places that are in a bit more remote location.

Vegan breakfasts and brunches can be difficult to find, particularly since a lot of vegetarian restaurants don't open until lunchtime. You're probably going to be doing a lot of walking and sightseeing so it's important to start the day off right with a hearty breakfast! Have a look and see if there are any vegetarian or vegan B&Bs, but if there aren't, don't give up. A lot of B&Bs are willing to make vegan breakfasts, so just ask before booking and see if they will accommodate you!

For example, I once stayed in a B&B in a rural part of the Isle of Wight. Now, this B&B was not only extremely beautiful, but they also made us an absolutely fantastic vegan breakfast. And it wasn't advertised on their site. My friend just emailed and asked if they could cook us a vegan breakfast. The owner was vegetarian herself, and she replied that she always had vegan sausages on hand. In the end, our multi-course breakfast included a fruit course, followed by cereal and soy yogurt course, followed by a full English fry-up.

Hostels

Hostels aren't just a budget-friendly option good for your wallet, they're also good for vegans! If you're not into sharing space with others, don't worry, most hostels have private rooms these days, and some have en-suite options too, if you want your own bathroom. Most hostels have kitchen facilities that are free for use, and which come equipped with pots, pans and even, sometimes, basic ingredients (oils, salt and pepper, even some spices). You might have to fight through a line in order to get your turn cooking, though.

The best places to look for hostels are Hostel World [hostelworld.com] and Hostel Bookers [hostelbookers.com], both of which will indicate whether a hostel has kitchen facilities. Or just email the hostel and ask before booking! Not only will having a kitchen mean you don't have to worry so much about finding food – you can always cook up something quick if needed (check out the recipes section for some ideas) – but it also means you can save some money while you're at it! Hostels tend to attract alternative types, and I've met many other vegetarians and vegans in hostels, so you might just meet some fellow vegans who can recommend places to eat.

When you check in to the hostel, ask about nearby grocery stories. Workers at hostels are used to getting asked this question, and will normally provide you with a free map with the nearby bus stops, supermarkets, and attractions marked. Then, you can go to a supermarket and pick up a few things to make sure you've got some snacks (like fruit, nuts, etc.) as well as some breakfast options. For breakfast, grab some cereal or oats and non-dairy milk, if they have it at the grocery (if not, check at a health food store). Most hostels with kitchen facilities will let you keep food in the fridge too – just make sure you write your name on it in marker pen, or someone may eat it!

Couchsurfing

I mentioned Couchsurfing as a way of finding other vegans and asking for advice, but it's also obviously a good option for finding places to stay (since that's what it was built for!). The concept of Couchsurfing is that you can find a sofa to stay on – free – just about anywhere, making travel more practical, but also allowing you to engage in cultural exchange. Instead of staying in a run-of-the-mill hotel, and never speaking to any locals, you can sleep in their house and learn about new cultures, as well as make new friends. Actually a lot of Couchsurfers are expats, so you may find that the "local" you're staying with isn't so local.

Couchsurfing isn't just couches (despite the name), so you might find yourself staying in a spare room, or on the floor. Usually the sleeping arrangements are noted in the host's profile, so you know what you're getting into. Keep in mind that Couchsurfing is about building community and learning about other cultures, and Couchsurfing hosts do not appreciate it if you are just looking for a free place to crash, and not interested in learning about new cultures.

It's considered polite to return the favor – not necessarily by hosting the people who hosted you, but by becoming a host yourself when you return home, or at the very least offering up your availability to take people passing through your city for coffee. (You can set on your profile what sort of availability you have – couch, if you've got somewhere for people to crash, or just coffee, if you don't have the capacity/don't want someone to stay in your house, but are willing to meet people and show them around.)

As we spoke about previously, you can use the keyword search in Couchsurfing to find other vegans and vegetarians. If you're staying with someone, you might want to find someone who's vegetarian or vegan, so you know they'll be able to recommend eateries to you and that they'll have vegetarian or vegan food in the house. If you don't mind, or can't find a vegan or vegetarian to stay with, you should still mention your dietary requirements to your host before you arrive (and be explicit about what it means, in case they aren't familiar with the concept or the English word), lest they prepare their grandmother's favorite lamb stew and try to feed you spoonfuls of it the moment you walk in the door.

A note on safety: Before Couchsurfing, read up a bit on safety concerns and make sure you know what you're getting yourself into. There have been reports of rape, assault and attacks, although there aren't many in comparison to the volume of Couchsurfing going on. Make sure you take precautions to protect yourself. Read reviews on the host, think about whether or not you want to stay with a single male/female, a couple, or a group, and consider what you'd do in case something bad did happen. Never, ever stay somewhere if you feel uncomfortable once you've met the person/set foot in their house. Always have the number/address of a hostel as a backup, and know how to get yourself there should you need to (e.g. know the public transport route or get the number of a taxi company).

Airbnb and Homeaway

If you haven't heard of Airbnb [http://airbnb.com], you've probably been living under a rock for the last couple of years! It's somewhat of a cross between Couchsurfing (well, a more upmarket version of Couchsurfing – you're paying, after all) and renting a flat, and hotel owners everywhere are up in arms because it's undercutting their profits with its popularity, which is why it's been splashed all over the news.

Anyone can sign up and put their flat (all or part of it) for rent. They might just rent out a spare room, in which case it's a bit like Couchsurfing or a B&B, or they might put up a whole spare apartment for rent. You can select when searching whether you'd rather see rooms to rent, or entire apartments, depending on whether or not you want to stay on your own/ have the whole apartment to yourself, and how much you want to pay. If staying in a room, you may want to email the host and mention that you're vegan, and find out whether you'll have access to the kitchen and/ or fridge – useful as a backup plan and place to cook and store your soy milk/snacks.

Homeaway [http://homeaway.com] is very similar, except that only entire apartments or houses are on offer (you can't rent just a spare room), and it tends to attract slightly more upscale apartment rentals (prices reflect this).

Be sure to read up on safety concerns (see the warning in the Couchsurfing section above) and take precautions to protect yourself, especially if you're staying in a spare room instead of renting an entire apartment. Also be aware that in some cities like Barcelona, Airbnb has come under fire from local renters, who complain that apartments are being turned into overpriced holiday rentals, thereby driving up prices for rentals being rented out to the local market. Some municipalities have even made Airbnb illegal, so be sure to research the legalities and local feelings toward Airbnb at your destination before deciding whether or not to use it.

Housesitting

One popular way of traveling, particularly amongst long-term travelers, is housesitting. If you haven't heard of housesitting, it's exactly as it sounds. You look after someone's house (and sometimes pets) while they're on vacation or sabbatical, often for free. It's an excellent way to travel for free, although I've heard it can be hard to get started. (Who wants to leave their house in the hands of someone completely new, without any reviews?) If you know anyone who does housesitting, you could ask them to help you get started, and possibly refer you to someone. Be sure to ask them for a good review! The most popular site is Trusted Housesitters [http://www.trustedhousesitters.com/], which costs $119 yearly (both housesitters and those looking for a housesitter for their house pay $119). If you're planning to use it for more than a few nights, you should make back your $119.

Vegvisits

A promising new site is Vegvisits [http://vegvisits.com]. It is similar to Airbnb, for vegetarians, vegans, and others with special dietary requirements. You can stay with local vegetarians and vegans, and will be able to search by diet (e.g. vegetarian, vegan, raw, gluten-free). Also, interestingly, you'll be able to search by what appliances they have in their kitchen (blender, juicer, food processor) – which could be incredibly useful if you like to start off your day with a green juice or a smoothie bowl! You can also rent a kitchen (in someone's house) for a day or more, so you could use this option if you're staying in a hotel but want to rent a vegan kitchen to make your meals.

Renting an Apartment

This is one of my favorite options. If you're staying somewhere for a week or more, you can usually rent an apartment at a decent price – less than a hotel – and sometimes it even works out at a similar price to a private room in a hostel. The longer you stay, the cheaper it is. Have a look on TripAdvisor [http://tripadvisor.com], Airbnb (remember to filter for whole apartments), and Homeaway. You might also want to look for local sites.

Don't assume that all apartments have ovens or even ranges. You could arrive to discover there's a hot plate-type setup (common in smaller apartments in some locations). If you're planning to use the kitchen much, you'll want to make sure it has an oven or at least a range, plus a refrigerator, a microwave, and maybe a freezer. Also, most places come with basic cooking equipment, cutlery and plates, but it's worth making sure! Check by emailing the owner and verifying what cooking facilities and equipment are available.

More than likely, you'll find your apartment options limited because of your budget and particular items on your "wishlist" (number of bedrooms, Wi-Fi access, kitchen facilities and location), but if you do somehow find yourself spoilt for choice, bust out that vegan restaurant map again on HappyCow/Google and see if you can nab an apartment near some vegan restaurants or stores!

* * *

Notes

Section 5:

Preparing for Your Trip.

So, you've decided where to stay, made a list of restaurants and vegan-friendly phrases and selected your sightseeing "musts.". Don't leave just yet! Once you've chosen a place to stay, your next step is picking what to pack! I'm not talking first aid kits here (pack one of those anyway, though). We're going to cover eco-friendly and vegan-friendly toiletries that are also travel-friendly. We'll be focusing on emergency food supplies to make your vegan travel easier. Plus we'll talk about eating on airplanes.

What to Pack: Toiletries

Ah, the toiletry bag, bane of every plane traveler's existence! Things have gotten a little bit complicated for those of us who fly with carry-ons, now that there are so many rules about what we can take on the plane – and how much of it. That's especially true for those of us who want to take eco-friendly and vegan toiletries, and can't just run to the nearest drugstore and buy a big pile of mini Colgate toothpastes and tiny bottles of Pantene. The easiest option is to simply buy some empty bottles that are travel-sized/TSA-approved, and fill them with your favorite shampoos, soaps etc. You can easily refill these before each trip, so you're not wasting lots of tiny plastic bottles.

Toothpaste, on the other hand, is more of an issue. You can't pick up refillable toothpaste tubes at your nearest drugstore, but you can order these refillable, BPA-free tubes on Amazon (also great for packing sunscreen!):

US orders: http://amzn.to/2jSta5n

Or, you can buy little tubes of Jason brand natural toothpaste:

US orders: http://amzn.to/2kRKFQP
UK orders: http://amzn.to/2kNN7Zx

I'd also highly recommend checking out the hair and body care products at Lush, if you have a store nearby or can order online. They clearly label which products are vegan, all their products are natural and many are made fresh. They have some non-liquid products like face soap/scrub in plastic tubs, solid perfumes, solid shampoo bars, bath bombs (solid balls which dissolve in water into bubbles), solid massage bars (which melt when heated to skin temperature) and more. These are great because you can stock up without worrying about going over your liquid limit! If you want to bring a treat along and are staying somewhere nice with a bathtub, Lush bath bombs and bath melts are excellent.

You might also want to check the contents of toiletries to ensure they are eco-friendly and free from parabens, sodium lauryl sulfate (SLS) and other ingredients which have been implicated in causing health problems as well as environmental problems (some studies indicate that SLS may have a toxic effect on aquatic life). Many organic and vegan products are paraben and SLS free, but it's best to double-check anyway as this is not always the case.

If you're planning to travel for a while, you might need to do laundry, so don't forget to pack some laundry detergent. I find the best way to do this is to buy those laundry tabs (the solid ones), which transport well and, again, won't take you over your liquid limit. Or, you could buy a multi-purpose liquid like Dr. Bronner's Castile soap, which you can use for just about everything – laundry, shower gel/soap, face soap, as dog shampoo, even toothpaste. Buy here: http://amzn.to/2kOVhEn

Warning: I've never used it as toothpaste and the idea freaks me out a little, but by all means, try it and see what you think! But be warned it will taste like soap! You can also use plain, old-fashioned baking soda as toothpaste.

If you're traveling longer term, you might find yourself running out of toiletries. Check if there's a Lush nearby. Lush has expanded to a lot of locations and countries now! Or look for a local health food store. You may be able to buy a brand of your favorite stuff from back home. Be prepared to pay a lot more, and be prepared for it to taste really different. When I was in Taiwan, I bought some vegan, organic toothpaste from a brand that I regularly buy back home. However, instead of tasting minty fresh, this stuff tasted of salt! It made for a really salty, strange toothbrushing experience!

If you're planning a trip to the beach or just walking around a sunny city, don't forget to protect your skin! Sun lotion can be loaded up with nasty animal products (not to mention being tested on animals) but you can easily find vegan sunscreen at health food stores or online. If you're in the US I recommend Jason Mineral Sunblock, Kiss My Face Sun Spray or Jason Kids Sunscreen. In the UK, I recommend Green People Organic Sun Lotion, Green People Children's Scent Free Sun Lotion or Superdrug's Solait brand (check each bottle as some Solait sun creams are vegan and others aren't, but all the vegan ones are clearly marked as such). Worldwide, I recommend Lush sesame sun lotion, powdered sunscreen or shower sunblock. Don't forget to pack a hat and also to protect your lips. I love Hurraw! SPF lip balm.

Jason Mineral Sunblock: http://amzn.to/2kRPIkf

Kiss My Face Sun Spray: http://amzn.to/2kp1u95

Jason Kids Sunscreen: http://amzn.to/2kRV8vD

Green People Organic Sun Lotion: http://amzn.to/2kP7g4L

Green People Children's Scent Free Sun Lotion: http://amzn.to/2kP3lER

Hurraw! SPF lip balm: http://amzn.to/2kRO6Hc

If you do get a sunburn (oops!), drinks lots of water to hydrate yourself, cool your skin and apply lotion containing aloe vera or try Lavera After Sun or Green People After Sun lotion.

Lavera After Sun: http://amzn.to/2kRZeUw

Green People After Sun: http://amzn.to/2kRKrJq

Keep pesky mosquitoes at bay with vegan-friendly bug repellants. If you're in the US, try Beat-It All Natural DEET-Free Spray or Jason Quit Bugging Me Spray. In the UK, I recommend Incognito Spray.

Beat-It All Natural DEET-Free Spray: http://amzn.to/2jSESgf

Jason Quit Bugging Me Spray: http://amzn.to/2kRSgiD

Incognito Spray: http://amzn.to/2kOX5gG

It can get hot, sweaty and...smelly in the sun if you're traveling to warmer climes. Don't torture your travel companions with your stinky pits, make sure you have some vegan deodorant on hand. In the US, try Jason's Tea Tree deodorant or Lavanila deodorant. If you're in the UK, I recommend Fit Pit, a vegan and chemical-free deodorant.

Jason's Tea Tree deodorant: http://amzn.to/2koMR5p

Lavanila deodorant: http://amzn.to/2jst0TH

Fit Pit: http://thegreenwoman.co.uk/

On a side note, when choosing clothes for your trip: Those "travel clothes" you often see travel magazines and blogs talking about (you know, the ones that wick moisture, never smell, don't wrinkle and pretty much sound like magical clothes that wash themselves) are not always vegan. They quite often contain silk, so check the fabrics of anything before purchase.

Need a cute bikini for your beach escape? Vitamin A swimwear makes swimsuits out of recycled nylon fibers, while Lisa Blue swimwear donates 25% of their profits to whale and dolphin protection.

What to Pack: Food

So if you're anything like me, you almost always have a few snacks buried in the bottom of your bag. You put them in there at some point thinking, "I

---

better pack some extras in case I can't find vegan food before my meeting/ near the museum/at Sam's party even though she specifically told me she'd be making vegan food for me." I don't know where this irrational fear came from because I've never actually been anywhere I can't find at least one vegan option (although it may be just a banana or a bag of nuts). I don't really think it has anything to do with a fear of being without vegan food, more of a fear of ending up in the countryside/in the middle of a zombie apocalypse without any food, period. It probably explains why my cupboards are stocked to the brim with a huge supply of beans, nuts and grains. Just in case one of those zombies, well, …you know. I'd definitely be the one of my friends whose house everyone would go to in order to survive. Anyway, I usually forget that I've stockpiled things in my bag, and whilst cleaning out my handbag, discovered a long forgotten stash of Nakd bars and bags of dried fruit and nuts. Oops.

It does pay, though, to bring a few emergency supplies with you on your trip, particularly in case of an unfortunate airplane incident. You know, one of those awful cases where they forget to bring your vegetarian or vegan meal even though you ordered it in advance. Don't risk digging to the bottom of your bag only to discover that somehow this is the one time you DON'T have any bars. So you end up eating some Pringles you picked up in the airport as a treat, along with a slightly melted dark chocolate bar you found at the bottom of your bag (not the best dinner) while the flight attendants cackle (honestly, cackle) in the corner like the evil stepmother in a Disney princess movie and make fun of your sorry, sorry excuse for a dinner. Oh wait, am I the only one that happened to? Well, suffice it to say, I learned my lesson and I now bring some food on all flights.

Yes folks, this happened. Generally, most airlines are pretty good with vegan meals, but this time they failed. Big time. When the flight attendants came over and explained they'd forgotten my special meal, they offered me the vegetarian option of lasagne – a cheese-filled lasagne. No way that was going to be veganized! I explained that I didn't eat dairy, and the flight attendants seemed confused, then told me they didn't have any food to give me. So, I ended up eating Pringles and chocolate while the flight attendants laughed at me and commented snarkily, "That's an interesting dinner." (Yes, I did complain, and the airline did apologize, but that didn't really make up for it.) Moral of the story: Have a couple of backup bars, or something more substantial than Pringles.

Having energy bars or snacks in your bag is particularly handy on cheap flights which don't provide meals. It also helps to avoid paying for excessively overpriced and often unhealthy meals in the airport. What's the key to packing a meal for the plane? Make something easily transportable, and also something that can be eaten cold, like a sandwich.

What should you bring with you? Preferably some non-perishable and filling foods, like meal replacement or energy bars (think Larabars, Lunabars, Clif bars, Nakd bars etc), dried fruits, nuts and seeds. Plus some foods that are easy to transport that won't go bad quickly, like a sandwich or wrap, pasta or sushi. You can bring these with you on the plane for dinner! If you want to go the extra mile, bring some vegan chocolate (just for a treat on the plane!) and powdered soymilk or creamer (so you can have coffee on the plane - also a bonus if you're not sure if you'll find soymilk at your destination, because the powdered version means you can still have coffee and even make soymilk for your cereal). Warning: make sure you bring the powdered soymilk in its original, unopened packaging, lest you raise the suspicion of security, who might want to know what your white powder is!

Not sure if you want to bring a sandwich on board? Try bringing something you can make easily in hot water (most planes have hot water for tea, so just ask nicely if you can have some for your food), lik instant oatmeal or instant soup. Just check the ingredients to make sure they're vegan. Hey, it may not be the healthiest option, but if you're desperate for something on a plane, it's better than nothing!

Need some ideas? Try making...
• Hummus + spinach + tomato wrap
• Peanut butter & jelly
• Tofu + roasted vegetable sandwich
• Pasta with roasted vegetable tomato sauce
• Sushi with avocado, cucumber and carrot
• Fruit that's easy to transport (apples, oranges, grapes etc. Don't try bringing peaches with you on a plane, they'll just get crushed!)
• Potato chips/crisps or crackers
• Trail mix of peanuts, cashews, sunflower seeds and pumpkin seeds (plus dark chocolate chips if you want) - nuts are great because they're small and light but pack a lot of energy
• Dried apples or dried cranberries

Remember not to bring any liquids or make sure that they are in smaller containers that won't take you over your liquid limit. And yes, airport officials often count "pastes" like hummus as liquid, as well as salad dressings.

You can make your own fruit and nut bars. Check out this super useful post from Oh She Glows with some great ideas and recipes for easily transportable snacks for the plane: http://bit.ly/1YplVxQ

Some airports also have a listing of different restaurants and stores by terminal, and you can use these to check if there are any places that you know have vegan options. For example, in UK airports there is often a Pret which offers a vegan sandwich option. There are branches of Chipotle in some US airports, which offers vegan burritos. The Physicians Committee for Responsible Medicine (PCRM) put together a great airport guide. While it's from 2015, much of it is still up to date. Find it here: http://bit. ly/pcrmairportguide

Depending where you're going, and whether you're staying in a place with a kitchen where you plan to cook, you may want to bring along a few foods as well. If you're planning to cook, have a look at supermarkets and health food stores nearby, and find out if there are any foods you'll want which will be difficult to obtain. A few things worth considering taking:

- UHT/shelf stable soy milk (either one carton as a "starter" soy milk, so you at least have some for the first day, or in single packs if you're not going to have a fridge. You can use these single servings for breakfast each morning!).

- Powdered non-dairy coffee creamer or powdered soy milk (if you're going somewhere without a fridge, or you know you won't be able to buy soy milk in the location you're going. At least you can still have creamer in your coffee!).

  US orders: http://amzn.to/2jSrQwY

  UK orders: http://amzn.to/2ko9Cqq

- Instant ramen. (Try and find the healthiest brand possible, for example Koyo which is organic, vegan, made without MSG, and sold in many health food stores in the US and on Amazon: http://amzn.to/2kRT9rd.) You can make this easily if you have a kettle in your hotel room, or your hotel provides hot water for tea.

- Dark chocolate or other treats (if you have a sweet tooth and are going somewhere you won't be able to easily get vegan desserts).

- Nutritional yeast – if you like cooking with it and are going somewhere you can't easily buy it.

- Spice mix – this might make your cooking easier.

  The last thing you'll want to do is buy a bunch of spices for a kitchen you're only going to be using for a short period of time. I'd suggest picking one style of cooking and bringing a spice mix that is versatile, for example I like taking an Italian spice blend with me and using it to make pasta, sauté veg and make risotto/toppings for polenta, etc. Or, you can buy spice mixes for specific dishes like these for sale in the US, which are organic and come with a shopping list of fresh ingredients to pick up (e.g. chickpeas, tomatoes, and ginger): http://amzn.to/1X8UOtQ.

- Or you can even make your own spice mixes in plastic bags and bring them with you (tip: make sure your plastic bags are really well sealed so you don't end up with spices all over your bags! And be prepared for potential questions at security if you pack dried oregano).

- If you want to go all out you can come extra prepared like this traveling kitchen kit as described by Joy the Baker: http://bit.ly/1T9Y81U

You may also want to bring a portable set of cutlery, like the kind you can get for picnics or camping. (Just remember to pack it in your checked luggage!) Other useful kitchen tools to have on hand are a Swiss army knife or kitchen knife for chopping vegetables, scissors, a can opener, a vegetable peeler, and a corkscrew. Again, these are sharp objects and must go in your checked luggage, not your carry-on.

Eating on the Plane

Almost all major airlines offer vegan meals these days (on flights that serve meals, that is). Shorter flights and domestic flights normally don't serve meals, so check your booking. They might sell sandwiches on short flights, but vegan options are few and far between. If you're on a flight that's serving meals, you'll need to book your meal when you book the tickets, or shortly thereafter, but at least 72 hours in advance. To be on the safe side, I recommend booking your vegan meal as far in advance as possible, and double-checking at the desk when you check in to make sure they have your dietary request in your booking.

First of all, you need to find out whether a meal is being served on your flight. If you're getting a flight within the continental United States (and newsflash: some airlines treat flights to Costa Rica and Hawaii, however long they are, as flights where they don't have to serve meals), you probably won't be served a meal. Likewise, on a budget flight in Europe such as Ryanair or Easyjet, you most likely won't be served a meal.

But if you're flying longer haul, you most likely will be served food. Some airlines, like China East or Aegean, serve meals even on flights as short as an hour. Check your reservation or ticket to see if it says food will be served. If it does, you'll need to order a vegan meal at least 72 hours in advance, although I'd recommend booking it earlier, just after you purchase your ticket.

You can usually request your meal on the airline's website (after you've signed in or input your flight details); if not, just give them a call. If you're booking through a travel agent, make sure they know your dietary preferences and triple check that they ordered a vegan meal for you. Be certain that the people with whom you are speaking understand the difference between vegan and vegetarian.

Airlines have codes for special dietary meals, ranging from Kosher to Halal to low- sodium meals. The code for vegan meals, in airline terms, is VGML. Remember those four letters! The airline representative might not know what vegan means, but they will know the code. Confusingly, different airlines seem to refer to VGML in different ways, so some airlines call it vegan and others "vegetarian non-dairy" (to differentiate it from Asian Vegetarian meals, which do contain dairy), while some call it "strict vegetarian".

Other meals (not offered by all airlines):
VJML: Vegetarian Jain Meal
VLML: Vegetarian Lacto-Ovo Meal (so when you're ordered a vegan meal make sure it says VGML, not VLML)
VOML: Vegetarian Oriental Meal
RVML: Vegetarian Raw Meal

Depending on the airline, the Vegetarian Jain meal and/or Vegetarian Oriental Meal may be vegan so it's worth asking when you call.

Just bear in mind that with the Vegetarian Jain and Vegetarian Oriental Meals, some airlines deem them vegan, while others define them as containing dairy.

You should always follow up after placing your order for a vegan meal, just to confirm, when you check in at the airport and also, if possible, after boarding the plane.

Remember:
1. Call the airline (or make a request via their website) for a vegan meal, or a meal with the code VGML.
2. When checking in at the airport, confirm that you have reserved the vegan meal. Sometimes, it will say on your ticket "special meal request."
3. If possible, check with a flight attendant just after boarding.

What to Expect
Okay, so you've ordered your vegan meal, you've confirmed it when checking in, and generally followed all the right steps like an A+ student (well done, you!). But what should you expect when your meal is actually delivered to your seat?

Usually, special meals are delivered before anyone else's on the plane (yay!), which means that you get to feel special, and also that everyone will be jealous and suddenly interested in your meal. Another big bonus is that your meal is usually hot, because it's just come out of the convection oven, and didn't have to spend any time going up and down the aisles before coming to you.

Most airlines rely on air service catering companies to prepare the meals. These companies make tens of thousands of meals at a facility near the airport, cook the food to partly done and then deliver it to the aircraft. Once it's on board, they cook the food to completion in a convection oven, and then add the condiments as they bring round the trays of food during the flight. Read that again: they add any condiments like sauces, salad dressings, margarine/butter etc. on the plane! What does that mean for you, and vegans everywhere? It means that most of the time (unless you get lucky and are flying with a very clued-up airline), you will be given non-vegan condiments! On the odd occasions when I've actually received vegan margarine, coffee creamer and salad dressings I've been thrilled - that's how rare it is. Nine times out of ten, however, I've been given dairy-containing margarine, or salad dressing with milk in it. I'd recommend against eating the condiments (and be wary of the bread, too, which is also added on board the plane). The bits of food that come in little containers (labeled VGML), like the main and the side salad are the parts of the meal that were prepared by the catering company, and these should be vegan.

What kind of food should you expect? Most likely, something bland and tasteless - but that's not necessarily the airline's fault, or the catering company's. Your tastebuds' perception and your sense of smell is altered by the altitude of the plane, so you actually can't taste as well when you're in the air - meaning that the food won't have much flavor to you! Although the fact that it is mass produced food stored for hours and then reheated on the plane probably doesn't help, either.

Typical meals you might expect on the plane? Pasta dishes with vegetables, curry with rice, or vegetables with couscous are some typical ones. Be forewarned that a lot of airlines don't tend to do vegan snacks or breakfasts well. If they're passing out snacks, they likely won't have a vegan option. Similarly, there aren't always vegan breakfast options. When there are, it will likely be something simple like a fruit salad. Also, for dessert with your dinner? Expect a fruit plate. Most airlines have some ways to go in terms of vegan fare on offer. With several airlines hiring Michelin-starred chefs and building special pressurized kitchens to simulate a flight environment (and therefore develop tastier food in it), it looks like at least airlines are trying to make better food - let's hope that they'll invest in higher quality vegan options, too!

What if you're flying first class? Unfortunately, the first class a la carte menu is usually off-limits, and you'll be served the same meal as those ordering a vegan meal in economy. (Airlines usually just prepare one meal for "special diets.") However, your meal will usually be plated better than in economy. You'll get real plates, bowls and cutlery, and alcoholic beverages if you want.

Remember:

Check and double-check with the airline that they've ordered your vegan meal. I always request a vegan meal when I book my ticket, check it again about a week before the flight and then check once more when I'm checking in for the flight at the airport.

Avoid the condiments unless you can tell for sure they're vegan. More than likely, any margarine, salad dressing or coffee creamer they've given you isn't vegan.

As we've already discussed, I also always recommend bringing snacks and food (especially easily portable food and snack bars) with you on flights, in case they forget your meal. It can happen, and you don't want to be stuck on a plane for 10 hours with only some potato chips to eat!

* * *

Section 6:

What to Do When You Get There.

. . . .

We've covered researching and finding restaurants, where to stay, and what to pack. This section is all about what to do when you get there – from making friends, to ordering at non-vegan restaurants, to what to do if you're traveling with non-vegans. This section will also cover picking vegan activities and what to do if you get stuck and can't find anywhere to eat.

Making Friends

Depending on how long you're staying in a locale, how long you'll be traveling (if you're going multiple places) and whether you're traveling with friends/a partner/family, you may be inclined to make friends on your trip. If you're traveling for a while, or you're on your own, you'll probably want to meet people – but no matter what your circumstances, arranging to meet like-minded people who live in your destination is a great way to make new friends and learn about local culture.

You can use some of the methods listed earlier, such as Couchsurfing and Meetup, to contact people with shared interests. Hostels are another classic way to meet people. Check reviews to see what sort of atmosphere the hostel has. Some hostels may be "party" destinations or have chilled hangout areas where you can meet people, while others tend to be used strictly for sleeping, with guests who are not very inclined to mix with others. As long as a hostel has a common area or a kitchen, though, you are likely to meet people.

You can also meet people on trains, or on walking tours (in many cities, you can find free ones, just Google or ask your hostel's front desk!). I've even met people in restaurants, when someone at a table nearby struck up a conversation – also a great way to meet local vegetarians and vegans! Keep an open mind and your best asset is a friendly smile. As long as you seem open, you don't necessarily even need to be outgoing – people will often just start conversations with you if you are traveling alone. If you're in a group, you'll likely need to make more of an effort to start conversations.

If You're Traveling with Non-Vegans

"Okay," you're thinking. "It's all well and good finding a list of amazing vegetarian and vegan restaurants I want to go to, and salivating over their menus. But my friends/grandma/boyfriend won't want to go there with me! They'll refuse and I'll be left to dine on lettuce in some meaty restaurant they choose!" You have three choices here:

1. Convince your meat-eater(s) to go to vegetarian or vegan restaurants
2. Go to non-vegetarian restaurants with them (and try to find vegetarian or vegan options)
3. Go for meals separately

Getting Your Travel Companion to Go to Veggie Restaurants

If your travel companion isn't familiar with vegetarian restaurants, start by taking them to restaurants before your trip. It's up to you whether or not you tell them in advance of the restaurant visit that it's a veggie place. If you think they'll feel "tricked" by you taking them to a restaurant and not mentioning it's vegetarian, you should mention in advance of the visit that it's a veggie place. Judge according to their personality! But no need to make a huge deal of the place being vegetarian. After all, it's just a restaurant – one that happens to be vegetarian or vegan.

Taking them to veggie places can work well, if you choose good restaurants, and convince them that maybe veggie/vegan food isn't so bad after all – in fact, it's downright delicious. Of course, you should take them to the best veggie restaurants you know. You might just need to go on a fact-finding mission and check out restaurants before you take them there. You want to show them the best of the best, after all, so they see that vegan food is tasty! By the way, offer to treat them to dinner and they're more likely to agree to visit the place with you. ;)

If your companions are the adventurous types, you can pitch going to veggie restaurants as a way to try out new things. They might just discover some new favorite foods. A lot of people might be scared of eating out at exclusively vegetarian restaurants but come round to it when they realise they're not missing out and veggie and vegan food is quite delicious.

If there aren't any vegetarian restaurants near where you live, have them over for dinner one night prior to your trip and make the best meal in your repertoire, to show them that vegan food can be tasty. Of course, skip this one if you're a hopeless cook who burns toast.

Go to Non-Vegetarian Restaurants with Them (And Find Vegan Options)

If they're really adamantly opposed to trying out vegetarian restaurants, you might find yourself a bit torn. In this case, you'll likely end up eating in non-vegetarian restaurants with them. Try and choose the most vegetarian-friendly ones in this case, if possible (e.g. ones with vegetarian and vegan options clearly labeled on the menu). In North American I find that VegGuide is the best resource for finding these veggie-friendly restaurants. If you can't find these sorts of restaurants listed on HappyCow or VegGuide, try choosing a cuisine that normally has vegan-friendly options. See the next section for an exhaustive list of different cuisines and typically vegan options. Or you can always call restaurants a few days in advance and ask the chef to prepare a vegan option just for you.

Once when visiting family friends in Poland, our friends arranged a completely vegan meal for us in a local restaurant. We had pierogi, borscht, the works – all thanks to them phoning ahead before we arrived!

Even if you find you're unable to convince your companion to go to vegetarian restaurants with you, that doesn't mean you can't share any vegan meals with them on your trip. If you stay in a place with a kitchen, cook them a kick-ass vegan meal one night.

Dining Apart

When you're really determined to try a particular vegetarian restaurant you've heard lots of positive things about, it can be frustrating if your travel companions don't want to try it. In this case, you might want to make a deal with them. Perhaps there's an activity they really want to do that you're not as fascinated by? I'm not saying do anything that would compromise your values, but if your partner desperately wants to visit the museum of ancient anchors made between 500 and 300 B.C., maybe you could make a deal that you'll go to that museum if they then accompany you to the restaurant of your choice in the evening. Or maybe you can convince your travel buddies to go to a vegan restaurant with you if it's your treat.

Also remember that just because you're traveling together doesn't mean you have to do everything together. You can go off on your own, or meet new vegetarian and vegan friends (from Couchsurfing/Meetup) and try out those vegan restaurants you're dying to visit. Sometimes it's good to get a break from your traveling companions, especially if you are traveling together for a long time and starting to get on each other's nerves!

How to Order at a Non-Vegetarian Restaurant

So, what if you have to go to a non-vegetarian restaurant, either because your traveling companions don't want to go to a vegetarian restaurant, or because you simply can't find any? Well first, choose the restaurant carefully, and try and choose a place where you are more likely to be able to find vegetarian and vegan options. Think: Italian, Indian, Chinese, Thai, Japanese, Ethiopian, Moroccan, Lebanese…

Second, be careful how you order. Be prepared to ask a set of questions, not just "is this vegan?" in case they don't know what vegan means. In Section 3, "Translations," we covered a list of common phrases and words to translate, so have these handy! You'll want to ask questions specific to the local cuisine. So for example, in India, ask whether a curry contains ghee – but no need to ask if it contains fish sauce (unless you're in a Thai restaurant in India).

Be aware that in some cultures, it's considered rude to say no, so they may lie and say yes, it is vegan – even if it's not. In some Asian cultures such as Thai culture, there's a strong culture of "saving face" which means it's considered bad form to say no. Read up on the local culture!

Don't assume that something is vegetarian or vegan just because it looks like it might be. Sometimes vegetable side salads will come garnished with cheese or bacon, even though that's not listed on the menu. Sometimes ramen may sound like it's all vegetable, but come topped with an egg, or be made with a stock that's not vegan. Make sure you ask questions.

However, don't be discouraged if the waiter says they don't have any vegetarian or vegan options – just ask whether they can make something for you! As long as you ask politely – and not in a demanding, expectant way – most restaurants are willing to adapt their dishes to make them fully plant-based (or even invent a new dish). Be appreciative of their efforts, and be sure to thank the restaurant staff for making a vegan dish! If the dish is really fantastic, write up a review on it afterwards, and consider submitting it to HappyCow!

Here are the five most important steps to ordering vegan food anywhere:

1. Be patient. You might have to explain a few times what vegan means, and you might have a conversation about how "just a *little* bit" of egg is not, in fact, vegan (actual conversation I had in a Japanese restaurant). You might also have to wait while your server speaks to the chef.

2. Be appreciative. If they do have vegan options, thank them and make sure you let others know – that way the restaurant will know there is a demand for vegan food!

3. ASK for vegan options. If the restaurant doesn't have any vegan or veganizable options, ask them to add some to their menu. If they have dishes that can easily be made vegan, ask them to add a vegan version to the menu!

4. Think outside the box (or burger bun). Seventy-seven percent of Americans report eating ethnic foods when eating out at least once a month, and many ethnic cuisines are much more vegan-friendly than traditional American restaurants. Plus, you get to explore different cuisines.

5. Ask the right questions, and know commonly vegan dishes. Don't just ask "is it vegan?" ask questions specific to the type of cuisine (e.g. "does it contain fish sauce?" in a Thai restaurant or "can you make it without ghee?" in an Indian).

Here are some common vegan dishes (plus the questions you should ask) in more than twenty-five different cuisines:

Burmese

Look for shan tofu noodle or soup. Shan tofu is a tofu made out of chickpeas. Also try tea leaf salad (made with tea leaves – and yes they're caffeinated, so don't have this before bedtime) and pennywort salad (a salad made with the pennywort herb).

Chinese

Stir fried vegetables and/or tofu are great bets. Ask if they're made with fish sauce or oyster sauce, and in the case of mapo tofu make sure they leave out pork as it's commonly made with it. If you're ordering vegetable fried rice, make sure to ask them to leave out egg. Last, when ordering a noodle dish, just ask them to swap rice noodles for egg noodles. Surprisingly, while in Chinese restaurants in the U.S. and Europe you'll usually find lots of vegetarian and vegan options, when in China you might have a lot of trouble in non-vegetarian restaurants. But don't worry, just look for restaurants attached to or near Buddhist temples; there are usually several all-vegetarian places.

Cuban

Look for rice and beans (check they're not made with lard or meat stock) with a side salad or fried banana.

Egyptian

Look for foul/ful (mashed beans often eaten for breakfast) and koshari (a mix of rice, pasta, chickpeas, lentils, noodles and fried onion).

Ethiopian & Eritrean

Ethiopian and Eritrean food are excellent for vegan options because traditional Orthodox Christians "fast" (eat vegan) on Wednesdays, Fridays and special holidays. See if you can get a selection of vegetable curries (make sure they are cooked without dairy) on injera (a special fermented Ethiopian flatbread made with teff flour that's spongy and lemony and is used as a spoon to scoop up bite of curry). Shiro (chickpea based curry), gomen (greens cooked with spices) and mesir wot (red lentils cooked with berbere spices) are delicious options.

French

French cuisine is notoriously difficult for vegans (and even vegetarians) but look for ratatouille, a classic stewed vegetable dish, olive tapenade made without anchovies or soup au pistou, a Provencal vegetable soup (just check if the pistou – pesto – contains cheese and if so, if they can leave it off).

Greek

Ask if they have "nistisimo" food (or fasting/Lent food, as traditional Greek Orthodox church followers eat vegan during Lent and before taking communion). Most accidentally vegan dishes are found in the mezze section of the menu (mezze are small plates, similar to tapas, and you can make a whole meal out of a few of these, usually without any raised eyebrows). Most food is made with olive oil rather than butter, but always ask if meat stock such as beef or chicken broth is used in cooking. For mezze, look for vine leaves stuffed with rice (make sure they don't contain or meat stock), fava (split pea dip), briam (eggplant/aubergine, zucchini/courgette, potatoes and peppers cooked in a tomato sauce), Greek salad without feta or gigantes (beans in tomato sauce).

Indian

Indian cuisine is incredibly vegetarian-friendly and with a few tweaks can be made vegan-friendly, too. You'll want to avoid any dishes with paneer (an Indian cheese), and ask for vegetable curry made without any milk products like cream. In particular ask them if they can cook your food with vegetable oil instead of ghee (clarified butter often used in Indian cooking). Have your curry with a side of boiled basmati rice and opt for chappatti bread (it's usually milk product free but just check) instead of naan which is almost always made with butter and/or yoghurt.

Indonesian

Try gado gado, vegetables with a peanut sauce (minus the crackers which usually contain fish). Or look for a meat-free nasi goreng, fried rice (but this fried rice is different from any fried rice you've had before – it's normally made with kecap manis, a sweet soy sauce, and served for breakfast). Always ask them to leave out the egg and the crackers (which usually contain fish).

Italian

Ask for pizza marinara (a naturally cheese-less pizza topped with just tomato sauce and garlic), or a veggie pizza without cheese. Just check that the crust is free of milk products. Or ask for pasta; ask for dried pasta, rather than fresh (usually contains eggs). Check that the sauce doesn't contain any animal products (sometimes they will add anchovies or pork). Look for pasta alla arrabiata (a spicy tomato-based pasta sauce) which is usually vegan. A lot of fruit gelatos are made without dairy (just ask).

Jamaican

Ital food (part of the Rastafarian movement) is almost always vegetarian and usually vegan. Look for boiled green bananas, mango chutney or callaloo, a steamed green.

It was boiling hot, mid August, and our first ever visit to Sicily.

My then boyfriend and I had just arrived, and after having stocked our holiday apartment with goodies from the nearby supermarket, we raced towards our destination: a vegan bar/cafe/restaurant I'd heard nothing but incredible things about. But when we arrived, we were sorely disappointed to see a sign outside saying it was closed for "ferragosto," or August vacations. Undaunted, we went to another nearby vegetarian restaurant that I'd discovered on HappyCow. It, too, was closed for ferragosto. One by one, we discovered that the handful of restaurants we had found on HappyCow were closed, as were the ones I'd selected from Palermo Vegetariana, a free Google map of vegetarian restaurants.

Palermo Vegetariana also listed some non-vegetarian restaurants, but none were Italian – and I really wanted to eat Italian food in Italy. I wasn't completely backed into a corner, because we had a kitchen in our rented apartment, so I had the option of cooking meals with delicious produce made from local markets. However, I did really want to eat out sometimes. I was on holiday, after all! I thought if worse came to worst we'd go to a restaurant and I'd enquire about vegan or veganizable options. We'd encountered so few people who spoke English, though, so I wasn't entirely convinced that I'd be able to get my point across.

Desperate, the next day I emailed the contact email listed on *Palermo Vegetariana*. I didn't receive a reply. I did, however, receive a Facebook friend request from someone in Palermo. To this day I'm not sure if it was the founder of *Palermo Vegetariana* (as I suspect) or a coincidence, but I accepted the request. Shortly thereafter, I was friended by a restaurant called Tartaruga (Turtle). I Googled the name and found page after page of articles describing the new restaurant (a slow food restaurant), which had only opened a few days before. Knowing that slow food restaurants are often vegetarian or have vegetarian options, I looked for some more information on Tartaruga. After digging a bit deeper, I discovered that Tartaruga was, in fact, fully vegetarian with vegan options.

I sent a Facebook message to my new restaurant friend on Facebook, asking if they were open that evening and if I could book a table for two and received a reply: "No English. Yes 19:00 table for tree [sic]." Slightly dubious but nonetheless curious, we set off for the restaurant at 19:00 and were greeted by Laura. Laura is undoubtedly the friendliest woman in the world and she welcomed us into her restaurant, and to Sicily, with open arms. Although she didn't speak much English, we were able to communicate enough by way of pointing at various dishes and asking "vegano?" That first night, she brought us free dessert and a sample of some vegan cheese she'd been working on (and hadn't yet put on the menu). We went back four more times during our visit. Also, the founder of Palermo Vegetariana finally replied to me and told me about one other vegetarian restaurant that was open, but told me pretty much everything else on the island was shut for August vacation. We visited the other restaurant but we were drawn back to Tartaruga, and especially Laura, over and over. She plied us with free food and drink, but it wasn't just that, or the fact that we wanted to support a new local vegetarian business – it was just that we felt so damn welcome!

Morning
Sicily, Italy
2013

Japanese

In Japanese restaurants in North America or Europe, look for kappa maki (cucumber roll sushi) or avocado maki (avocado roll sushi), and ask for the sushi to be prepared without mayonnaise. Also look for inari, thin fried tofu 'skin' stuffed with rice, and edamame (boiled soybeans served with sea salt). Other menu items to look for: miso soup (just make sure they don't use bonito fish powder), agedashi tofu (deep-fried tofu with a dipping sauce; just check the batter doesn't contain egg and ask them not to add bonito fish flakes to the dipping sauce or on top of the tofu), gyoza (dumplings; ask if they can stuff them with vegetables and leave out any meat such as pork, also check the dough doesn't contain egg) and udon noodles (a wide, flat wheat noodle; check the soup stock doesn't contain any fish or meat). Similarly to China, it's tricky to find vegetarian food in restaurants in Japan. Don't even bother trying to go into a non-veggie place and ordering vegetarian or vegan. They don't like modifying food, and put bonito fish flakes in loads of unexpected places. Like China, look for vegetarian restaurants (they're usually near Buddhist temples), which will be happy to accommodate you!

Kebab shop

Often kebabs have falafel – check if they can make you a falafel wrap (ask if they've fried the falafel in separate oil to any meat). Just make sure the bread doesn't contain dairy and ask them to hold the sauce if it contains dairy.

Korean

Try bibimbap (rice with vegetables and spicy chilli sauce) – just ask them to leave out meat and eggs. Also look for japchae, sweet potato noodles stir fried with vegetables – ask them to leave out meat (it's often made with pork). Kimchi, a spicy fermented cabbage and vegetable dish often served as a side, sometimes contains fish (oyster sauce, fish sauce or shrimp sauce) so check.

Lebanese (& other Middle Eastern cuisines)

I realise that there are big differences between Middle Eastern cuisines but for our purposes, a lot of Middle Eastern restaurants in the US, UK and Europe offer many of the same dishes. Look for falafel (spiced chickpea patties), hummus and tabbouleh (a salad made with copious amounts of parsley, bulgur wheat and chopped tomatoes and cucumbers). Other usually vegan options (check they're made without dairy) include batata harra (spiced potatoes), fattoush salad (a salad with crispy bread topping and lemony dressing) or muhammara (a spicy hot pepper dip found in Syrian and Turkish cuisine).

Malaysian

Malaysian food is a mix of different influences, from Indian to Chinese to European. Try popiah, spring rolls, and for them to be made without meat, shrimp, egg or lard. Also look for meat-free mee goreng, fried noodles, and make sure to specify no egg and ask them to use rice noodles in place of egg noodles. Also keep an eye out for vegan laska, a spicy curry soup (a rarity but worth asking for this delicious dish), without any meat or fish, shrimp paste or fish sauce.

Mexican

The classic vegan option is a meatless burrito with beans (check they're not made with lard or meat stock), rice (make sure it's not cooked in chicken stock) and vegetables, hold the cheese and sour cream. Guacamole is traditionally vegan but check (some places add yoghurt or sour cream). When venturing into other territory, such as tostadas, quesadillas or flautas, always make sure no cheese or lard is used. But beyond these 'standard' options try some exciting dishes like tacos made with rajas (roasted pepper strips), potatoes, nopales (cactus) or huitlacoche (a fungus that grows on corn and is now considered a delicacy). Just make sure the tacos are made without cheese.

Moroccan

From what I've heard, eating vegetarian in Morocco isn't always easy, but at Moroccan restaurants in North America and Europe, you can often count on finding some vegetarian and vegan options. Try zaalouk, a traditional salad made with eggplant/aubergine, tomato and garlic, loubia (white kidney beans cooked in tomato sauce), vegetable tagine and/or vegetable couscous. Just make sure they cook your food with vegetable stock and not meat stock.

Nepalese

Always ask for vegetarian dishes to be prepared without dairy, because dishes are often cooked with ghee (clarified butter) and paneer (a soft cheese) is sometimes used. Look for vegetable momos, fried dumplings, and dal baht, curried lentils over rice.

Peruvian

Peruvian food is not traditionally very vegetarian- and vegan-friendly, but look for a version of rocotto relleno, stuffed pepper, made with onion and garlic as stuffings (as opposed to cheese or meat), papas a la ocopa (boiled potatoes in a peanut sauce – ask them to hold any cheese which is sometimes served as a side), ensalada de pallares (a butter bean salad – ask them to leave out fish), solterito (a choclo corn salad – ask them to leave out cheese) and sopa de verduras (vegetable soup – just make sure it's made with vegetable stock and they don't add any chicken or dried meat).

Pizzeria

Ask for a veggie pizza without cheese (and since they're taking the cheese off, ask if you can have something extra, like more mushrooms or some walnuts). Check that the crust is free of animal products, especially milk products. Avoid pesto as it usually contains dairy.

Sandwich/wrap shop

Ask if the bread contains any dairy. Ask for a wrap with vegetables. Ask what sauces they have – if you're in luck they might have hummus.

Spanish/Tapas

Most dishes are cooked in olive oil (not butter). Look for pimientos de padron (fried peppers with sea salt), tomato bread (crusty bread grilled and rubbed with garlic, tomato and finished with a drizzle of olive oil), gazpacho (cold tomato soup, not a traditional tapa but an excellent vegan Spanish dish), patatas bravas (fried potatoes in a spicy sauce, ask them to hold the aioli as it often contains eggs, and check the bravas sauce doesn't contain any dairy), escalivada (roasted eggplant/aubergine, onion and peppers on toast) or espinacas con garbanzos (spinach and chickpeas).

Steak house

It sounds weird but you can often get a vegan meal here. Ask if they have baked (jacket) potatoes and if their side vegetables, such as broccoli or corn, can be cooked without butter.

Thai

Order a vegetable curry or soup, and just ask them to leave out fish sauce, oyster sauce or shrimp paste. Spring or summer rolls (make sure they're all vegetable and the dipping sauce doesn't contain any fish sauce) and raw papaya salad (no fish sauce or dried shrimp) are great options. For pad thai, make sure they leave out the egg.

Vietnamese

Summer rolls (ask for all-vegetable rolls and make sure the dipping sauce doesn't contain fish sauce) are fantastic, as is pho, a famous Vietnamese soup. Make sure the pho is made with vegetable stock (not a fish or meat stock) and doesn't contain any fish sauce. Banh mi sandwiches are also delicious vegan options; ask for a tofu or vegetable sandwich without any mayo or fish sauce.

Vegan Volunteering

When traveling, you'll probably want to make sure your activities align with your values. This means evaluating situations carefully. For example, you'll want to avoid some activities which are incredibly cruel: Thailand's famous tiger visits and elephant rides, visits to Seaworld, circuses or zoos in other cities. If you want to see animals in the wild, for example on safari, evaluate the program carefully to make sure it's cruelty-free, and the animals really are wild and allowed to roam free. You may want to even go a step further, and combine your travels with supporting and helping animals abroad. For example, you could volunteer in an animal sanctuary, donate to a local animal charity, or volunteer to help out at this elephant sanctuary in Thailand: http://www.elephantnaturefoundation.org/go/park.

You could also donate to an eco charity or offset your air miles. (Check that the offset program is doing what they state they are doing!) Or better yet, see if you can do the journey by train.

What to Do If You Get Stuck

Sometimes, no matter how many restaurants you look up before your trip, no matter how many maps you memorize or menus you know by heart, circumstances conspire against you.

If you run into trouble with your quest for a vegan meal, don't lose hope. As my experience in Sicily with Laura goes to show, if you reach out to your network, you can often find some vegan places, plus some wonderful surprises, kindness and even friendship.

I find that one of the best things about travelling as a vegan is that once you meet another vegan you feel connected as part of the vegan community. More often than not you are welcomed with open arms and taken care of. I'll never forget Laura's hospitality in Sicily.

So what's the best thing you can do if you're stuck? As stated previously, reach out to anyone in your network and make a connection to find someone local who's vegetarian or vegan. Even if you don't know a local vegetarian website, look for vegetarians or vegans on social networks (Facebook, Twitter), Couchsurfing, etc. Ask your connections if they know of anyone (you might find a friend of a friend of a friend). Try to find a local health food store, or if there aren't any, try to find an area of town where alternative types hang out, like near a university, and you might have more luck. This is also why it's helpful to stay somewhere with a kitchen. But if you don't have one, then go into local restaurants and explain that you're vegan (or show them a translation in the local language) and what you can and can't eat. Most people in most places in the world will help out if they can!

And if you're really stuck and can't find vegan food anywhere, check out the recipes in Section 9, some of which can be made with just a coffeemaker, or without any equipment.

* * *

Section 7:

Vegan Adventures.

. . . .

Sometimes you just need a little adventure in your life. Here's how to do it, vegan-style. Whether you're camping, road tripping or going on a cruise, here's how to plan your next vegan adventure. In this section, we'll talk about what to bring camping, how to pack for a vegan road trip, choosing a vegan-friendly cruise, looking for a retreat and finally, vegan tour groups you can join on your next adventure.

Camping

If you're planning to get out, have an adventure and sleep under the stars, you might be wondering what on earth a vegan can take camping. Rest assured, you won't starve at the campfire this year!

Some foods to take with you:
• Veggie burgers or sausages to cook on the campfire
• Vegan marshmallows (pick them up from your local health food shop) to toast over the fire
• Corn: wrap in aluminum foil and roast over the fire
• Pre-chopped vegetables (or bring vegetables and a cutting board and knife) to make vegetable kabobs
• Fresh fruit
• Dried fruit and nuts and/or your favorite fruit and nut bars (great because you don't have to worry about keeping them in a cooler or them going bad)
• Baked beans and a saucepan to cook over the fire – they make a great breakfast over some bread!
• Oats (or instant oat packets – check that they're vegan) and a saucepan to make oatmeal for breakfast
• UHT (non-refrigerated) plant-based milk
• Bread and peanut butter – peanut butter sandwiches are quick and easy!
Make sure you leave the campsite as you found it – animals like their habitat to be kept clean and not disturbed!

Looking for camping gear? Check out this incredibly handy list of vegan sleeping bags, thermal jackets, hiking socks and boots and more: http://www.veganoutdooradventures.com/gear/

Want to camp with others and make new friends while you're at it? Check out the annual Vegan Camp, held each year in the UK from late July to mid August. Find out more information at vegancamp.co.uk. Unfortunately there's nothing similar in North America at this time (unless you start your own!).

Cruises

Gone are the days of limp salad being the sole vegan option on cruise ships. These days all-vegan cruises are springing up, plus a number of major cruise lines now offer vegan options, too.

If you want to join an all-vegan cruise:
In the last couple of years, a number of all-vegan cruises have started. Cruise in style and rest assured that you'll have gourmet vegan food available.

Vegan Cruise: Billing themselves as the world's first vegan ocean cruise, Vegan Travel's Norwegian Fjords cruise will take place between September 25th and October 2nd, 2017. The cruise is 100% vegan, so you can expect delicious, all-vegan cuisine on board. Website: vegancruises.eu

Raw Vegan Cruise: After the success of the world's first raw vegan cruise in summer 2016, the raw vegan cruise returns twice in 2017, June 24th to July 1st and August 12th to 19th. The August cruise is kid-friendly. Both cruises will be in the Mediterranean, stopping at various locations in Croatia. Expect the cruise to include yoga, swimming and of course raw vegan food! Website: thewholelifestyle.com/raw-vegan-cruise

Vegan River Cruises: After several years of successful cruises, the vegan river cruise line is becoming established in the vegan cruise world. The river cruises usually take place on the Danube and of course include gourmet vegan food. For upcoming trips check their website: veganrivercruises.com

For vegan options on non-vegan cruise lines:
Traveling with a non-vegan who's not so keen on going on an all-vegan cruise, or want to go somewhere not reachable on the current vegan cruise lines? Don't fret, some non-vegan cruise lines have started offering vegan options on their ships!

Sea Dream Yacht Club: one of the menu options is a completely vegan, raw menu, created in conjunction with the Hippocrates Health Institute, and includes options such as Asian cashew curry salad, raw vegetable lasagne and cashew lemon cheesecake. Website: www.seadream.com

Holland America Line: HAL offer a vegetarian menu which has vegan options clearly marked. Vegan options include pad thai, vegetable jambalaya and a mezze plate. Website: www.hollandamerica.com

The following cruise lines offer vegan options on certain routes. Contact them to check:
Regent Seven Seas Cruises: rssc.com
Oceania Cruises: oceaniacruises.com
Disney Cruise Line: disneycruise.disney.go.com
Silversea: silversea.com

Road Trip

Planning a road trip or driving to your destination? Pack your car full of animal- free snacks so even if you're driving through the desert or cornfields, you'll have vegan food on hand! Here are ideas on how to stock your car, plus how to find vegan food at chain restaurants (so you can grab some food even when you stop off to buy some petrol).

Snacks to stock your car with:
• Chopped fruit and veggies (e.g. carrot sticks, apple slices, grapes) that are easy to eat in the car
• Sandwiches or wraps (best if you have a cooler to keep them in)
• Dips for your veggies or for bagels/bread, e.g. hummus or veggie pâté
• Corn chips and salsa
• Dried fruit and nuts
• Crisps and crackers
• Popcorn (already popped, of course!)
• Plenty of water and juice to keep you going
• Chocolate or other treats – if you feel like baking before you head off, make something easy to transport like muffins or cookies

Re-stock your snack supply at supermarkets along the way!

If you know where you're going to be staying each night, look up vegan and vegan-friendly restaurants in the area on Happycow.

Or choose chain restaurants that have vegan options. For a US list, see http://bit.ly/2ksgwuB.

For a UK list, see http://bit.ly/2ksmRpZ.

US road trippers can download the Vegan Xpress app (iOS, $1.99), which lists vegan options at chain and fast food restaurants.

Retreats

Maybe you just want to get away from it all... If you want to go on a retreat, vegan-style, check out some of these options.

The Farm (Philippines): a raw vegan retreat and wellness centre, the Farm has a range of different retreat options you can book, from the wellness retreat to stress management to fitness. Website: thefarmatsanbenito.com

Olive Retreat (Spain and Thailand): at Olive Retreat you will find yoga, meditation and vegan food in the olive fields in Andalucia, Spain or the beaches of Khao Tao, Thailand. Website: oliveretreat.com

Yoga Detox Retreats (Italy, Turkey, Portugal and Morocco): The yoga detox retreat offers a chance to escape from your daily stresses, practice yoga and, of course, eat healthy food. The retreat in Italy offers raw vegan food, while Portugal, Morocco and Turkey are juice fast retreats. Website: yogadetoxretreats.co.uk

Vegan Festivals

Every year, hundreds of vegan festivals and fairs are held in cities around the world. Most contain a lot of stalls selling street food, cakes, ice cream, drinks, packaged food (plus plenty of samples), vegan makeup, soap, candles, shoes, bags, t-shirts and much more. Plus there are usually speakers, panel discussions and sometimes you'll even find live music and stand-up comedy.

Why not plan a road trip to a vegan festival this year? You can find a list of vegan festivals around the world here: vegan.com/festivals. Some of the biggest vegetarian and vegan festivals held each summer include VegFoodFest Toronto, VegFest Bristol, UK, VeggieFest Chicago and Vegan Summer Festival Berlin, Germany.

A completely different kind of veg festival takes place in Thailand annually. The Phuket Vegetarian Festival (also called the Nine Emperor Gods Festival) is a religious festival held every autumn in the belief that abstinence from meat will help promote health and peace of mind. In addition to a huge array of vegetarian and vegan food being available all over the city, some participants self-mutilate by firewalking or piercing their cheeks with swords to appease the gods.

Tour Groups

Let someone else do all the planning for you and join a vegan tour group. Sit back and enjoy the sights, with all vegan meals taken care of for you. Just like a non-vegan tour group, in most cases you'll be expected to take care of your own airfare to and from the destination, but all your accommodations and (vegan) meals will be included in the price. Extra optional excursions (such as a tour of a Venetian glass factory) might cost more.

Vegan Travel Club: Ever wanted to explore the vegan offerings of Italy, Peru, the Dominican Republic or Puerto Rico with other vegans? Join a Vegan Travel Club tour. Website: https://vegantravelclub.com/?ref=19 (That's an affiliate link, so if you book your tour through that link, I'll get a small fee, at no extra cost to you.)

Veg Voyages: For years, Veg Voyages have offered cruelty-free, green and vegan adventure tours. In 2017 and 2018, Veg Voyages have trips planned for India, Malaysia, Thailand, Laos, Sumatra and Bali. Website: vegvoyages. com

Teen VGN Summer Camp: This is summer camp, vegan- style! For teens exclusively. Taking place in August at Margam Discovery Centre in Wales, UK. Website: teenvgn.com/camp

Vegan Camp: Another vegan summer camp for kids, this one taking place in California every summer: vegancamp.org

Vegan Surf Camp: Do you love surfing, or want to learn how? Then this vegan surf camp on the southwest coast of France, is for you! At surf camp, you'll find camping and a vegan organic kitchen preparing fresh meals daily. Also available: yoga classes, cooking workshops, beach games, movie nights on the beach and ping-pong competitions. You can book by the week, whichever week suits you best between the 24th of June until September 2nd, 2017. Website (English version): uk.vegansurfcamp.com

Last, if you don't want to join a tour group but want someone else to help you with your planning, order the Vegan Trip Planner Service from The Vegan Word. The Vegan Trip Planner service is perfect if you're too time-crunched to research your destination in-depth. Tell us your destination and requirements and we'll research and write you a vegan itinerary to the city of your choice: https://theveganword.com/trip-planner/

* * *

Section 8:

Special Considerations.

• •

Whether you're traveling with a dog, going abroad with your kids, planning a trip for those with allergies or looking for some advice on staying healthy while traveling, this section's for you. We'll discuss dog- and kid-friendly travel, traveling with allergies (to gluten, nuts) or special diets (raw vegan), and last we'll go over some healthy travel tips.

Dog-Friendly Travel

Don't want to leave your furry friend behind when you go on vacation? There's no need, as more and more places are becoming dog-friendly. My dog Benito (pictured in the photo) is becoming a seasoned traveler and so far has been to Spain, Croatia, France, the UK and the US.

Hotels

Find dog-friendly hotels and B&Bs on BringFido.com, or search on Tripadvisor and Hotels.com. On Tripadvisor, check the "Pets Allowed" box under Amenities. On Hotels.com, check the "Pet Friendly" box under Facilities. Always call the hotel and double check pets are allowed and check whether you'll need to pay an additional pet deposit. Some hotels limit the weight and size of dogs allowed to stay in the hotel. Find out if there are any special rules or restrictions. For example, some hotels won't let you leave pets in the room unattended.

Restaurants

So, what if you really want to include Bailey in all aspects of your trip, including your restaurant visits? A lot of restaurants and bars will let you bring your dog to their outside seating areas, if they have a terrace, beer garden or patio seating, and some will even provide a water bowl for your dog. You can search for restaurants on BringFido.com, or in the UK free app Doggity allows you to search for dog-friendly restaurants, cafes and pubs nearby.

Activities

Of course, if you're bringing Max on vacation, you'll want to know some dog-friendly activities you can do together. Parks, beaches (check which beaches are dog-friendly) and hikes are popular. I've heard rumors that some museums in Vienna allow dogs, but generally you'll want to consider outdoor activities for your canine bestie.

Car and Air Travel

Okay, now you know what to do when you get there, but what about getting from point A to B? If you're planning a road trip, make sure you have a car harness/seatbelt or bag that can be seatbelted in. Of course, you should never leave your dog unattended in your car, especially if it's hot outside! If you're using a travel bag or crate, make sure your dog is familiar with it and crate trained well before your trip. To make their trip more comfortable, put a t-shirt in the crate that smells like you (in other words, use one of your stinky, dirty t-shirts, not one fresh out of the wash).

What about if you're flying? Small dogs can often fly in the cabin with you (in a secure carrier, under the seat). Rules depend on the airline but most airlines have a weight limit plus restrictions on the size of the carrier, so check with the airline. You might also have to purchase a ticket for your dog (don't worry, these are usually a lot less expensive than a human ticket!). Make sure your dog is trained and comfortable in the carrier before you leave. Bigger dogs may have to travel cargo, which can be risky so you'll want to research this option and weigh whether your dog has to make the flight. Some breeds (snub-nosed breeds like pugs) are not always allowed to fly because it can be difficult for them to breathe in the plane. Visit your vet before you fly and discuss your individual's dog's needs, plus how to prepare your furry friend for the flight.

What to Pack

I once read an article by someone whose dog has her own suitcase! While that's not necessary, make sure you bring everything you need to make Bella comfortable. You'll want to make sure you pack her harness, leash, enough food to last the trip*, treats, waste bags, brush, dog shampoo (in case you go to a park and find yourself in a muddy situation), a travel carrier, medicine, collapsible water bowls or a portable water bowl for long walks and all the proper papers/certificates. That means rabies certificates, an EU pet passport, etc. depending on where you're headed.

*If you can't pack enough food for the whole trip, make sure you know somewhere you can re-stock, or if not, have a plan in place for transitioning her to new food (dog's stomachs can get upset if you switch their food quickly). If your dog is vegan, it's especially important you bring enough food for the duration of the trip as it can be hard to get vegan dog food in some places. If you do run into trouble, try contacting a local vegan organization and asking if they know where you can buy vegan dog food (this worked for me in Croatia)!

If you're traveling abroad and your phone won't work, get your dog an ID tag with your email address printed on it. Or if you can get your hands on a SIM card and a local number, bring some luggage tags with you and write your local number on the luggage tag and tie it onto your dog's harness or collar.

Recommended websites

pettravel.com : Information on immigration, pet passports/international travel documents, airline pet policies and more.

montecristotravels.com : Recommendations for pet-friendly accommodation, activites and more.

dogjaunt.com : Small dog travel, airline reviews, recommendations for airline-approved carriers.

Kid-Friendly Travel

Traveling with kids, especially abroad, can open up an entirely different side of a place. Locals are more likely to engage with you if you have a cute tot in tow. You're also going to see sights you might not see otherwise, like playgrounds, child-friendly museums and more. Seeing a location through your youngster's eyes might just open up your vision to details you wouldn't have noticed otherwise.

Flying with children

The most nerve-wracking part of traveling with children is flying. Make sure you have plenty of snacks, breast milk or formula packed. The last thing you want is a cranky, hungry child. Make sure you have plenty of food on hand, too, in case the airline forgets your meals. Breast milk and formula are exempt from TSA travel restrictions on liquids, but agents may need to inspect the containers and perform extra security checks.

If you've got a toddler or small child, bring plenty of kid-friendly snacks. And make sure they are airline-friendly too (not liquids or pastes like hummus, which are restricted to the 3.4oz/100ml limit imposed by the TSA). Carrot sticks, grapes, apple slices (sprinkle with lemon juice to keep them from browning), nuts and dried fruit are good options.

If you're worried your kid may cry and disturb other passengers, you can always bring a few treats like chocolates, small bags of crackers or candies to pass out to the people seated near you. You might just make some friends on your flight!

Make sure you allow plenty of extra time because it can take longer to get through an airport with a curious child who wants to stop and examine everything. And pack some coloring books, small games or children's books so they have plenty to do on the flight.

Road Trips

Traveling by car can be easier with kids than flying, but make sure you allow plenty of time for bathroom breaks and don't try to drive too many hours in one day. Learn some car games (like I Spy) and pack plenty of toys.

Bring a cooler so you can pack snacks and meals for the car, especially if you'll be driving through areas without many vegan options. Refer to Section 9 for some easy recipes you can whip up in a hotel room. Sandwiches, crackers, fruit, nuts and carrot or celery sticks are easy to pack. You can replenish your cooler's ice supply from ice machines at hotels along the way.

Safety

Make sure your kids carry a card with the name and address of the hotel you're staying at in case they get lost. If you're going on the metro or train, make sure they know what station to get off at in case you get separated. If your child has a history of wandering off, you can buy devices called child locators; these are small units which strap to a belt or shoe. If you lose them, you can press the transmitter (which you should hang onto at all times) and the unit will emit a beep, which allows you to find your child by following the noise.

Be sure to pack any medicine your child takes, as well as any medicines that you might need, such as cough or cold medicine and pain relief. And make or buy a first aid kit to take with you!

General Tips

Engage older kids by letting them help you plan the trips, such as choosing some activities or picking between different restaurants. Older kids might also enjoy keeping a travel journal to record the trip.

If you're going on a longer trip or abroad, start learning about the history and culture of your destination before your trip. Kids love visiting places they've read about!

Travel with Allergies and Special Diets

So, you've got a special diet beyond being vegan? You're also allergic to tomatoes, coconuts and mushrooms?

Whatever your allergies or restrictions, don't let it stop you from traveling. One of my friends has been allergic to all nuts since she was a child; she was told never to travel in Asia, but moved to Thailand, where she lived for four years.

We're going to discuss how to travel with allergies (whether that's to gluten, nuts or anything else). Then we'll talk about special diets, like how to plan your vacation if you're a raw vegan or on a whole foods diet.

Allergies

Your translations are your best friend! If you have allergies, it's super important that you make a list of phrases/questions and translate them into the local language. As we talked about before, you should have a list of phrases prepared before your trip regarding vegan food (ex. "I am vegan," "Does this contain dairy?" and "I don't eat meat, fish, eggs or dairy products"). If you have allergies, you NEED to bring translations with you that clearly state your allergy in English and the local language(s). For example:

I am allergic to corn.
I am allergic to peanuts and tree nuts.
I am allergic to gluten / I am celiac.

You might also want to include pictures (e.g. a drawing of nuts with an X through it). You can find these online by googling your allergy.

Plenty of countries are becoming Celiac-friendly and offering gluten-free fare. Even Italy, the home of pasta, has more and more gluten-free pasta available! A lot of vegetarian and vegan restaurants are aware of allergies and offer gluten free and soy free food, but since many are small establishments they might not be able to ensure there's no cross contamination, so it's best to call in advance and check what they can offer you.

If needed, you should carry two epi pins and have them with you at all times. Carry all other medical equipment and a medical card stating your allergies (you might want to put this in your wallet).

Check with the airline before booking to see if they can provide an allergy-free meal; if not, bring your own food. Airlines also have information about whether they serve peanuts and tree nuts; you might want to choose an airline that doesn't serve tree nuts if you have a severe allergy to them.

More information on traveling with allergies here: foodallergy.org/managing-food-allergies/traveling

Special Diets

As discussed in the Allergies section, if you're traveling and have a special diet, you'll want to make sure you have translated phrases handy. In addition to phrases about vegan food, you should translate some phrases about your specific dietary requirements, such as "Is this raw?" or "Do you have any raw vegan food?"

More and more raw food restaurants and health-conscious eateries are springing up around the world. Go into any major city in North America or Europe and you'll probably find a few raw food places.

Before your trip, have a look at the restaurant listings on HappyCow for your destination. Most will note if they offer any raw or whole foods dishes.

If it doesn't seem like your destination offers many raw/whole foods restaurants, you might want to look into renting an apartment with a kitchen or a hotel with a mini kitchen (or renting a vegan kitchen on VegVisits, where you can even search for kitchens with equipment like juicers and food processors).

Order Allergy Cards

You can order allergy cards or diet cards (or even special cards) translated into the language of your choice for $14.95 here: www.selectwisely.com

These are small, pocket-sized cards you can slip into your pocket, bag or wallet to present to servers.

A Final Note

Whether you're traveling with allergies or a special diet, it's especially important you bring some food with you (though I recommend this to all vegan travelers!). While you can find fruit and vegetables everywhere in the world, you never know when your plane will get stuck on the tarmac for four hours while everyone becomes progressively more hungry and cranky.

Make sure you pack easy to transport fruit or veggies, nuts or bars like Nakd bars, which are raw bars made of just fruits and nuts. (Or make your own bars!)

Healthy Travel

You spend a lot of time at home making sure you eat organic, local whole foods and you train for marathons, so you don't want to lose your healthy edge while traveling, right? Because even vegan travel can offer plenty of temptations, like that persimmon gelato you just have to try or those deep-fried vegan Mozzarella balls that are screaming your name.

But you can maintain your healthy lifestyle while traveling.

Finding (or making) healthy food

Most vegetarian and vegan restaurants offer at least a few healthy options, unless you go to a vegan fast food place. Phone ahead or look up menus online in order to ensure that the places you're heading to offer some healthy fare.

Keep some healthy snacks in your bag, like fresh fruit or nuts, so that you're never so ravenous you're tempted to throw aside your healthy diet for a slice of cheeseless pizza.

If you do end up straying, don't fret. Just make sure you only splurge on things that are really worth it. Or, split the dish with your travel companion and order something healthy to go with it! But you're on vacation, so it's okay to indulge every once in awhile, especially on the kinds of unique food you can only order in your destination, like authentic dairy-free fruit gelato in Italy.

Try to book a holiday apartment or hotel with a kitchen for at least part of your stay, so you can prepare some healthy meals during your trip. You could even make a few portable meals and have a picnic!

Drinks

Make sure you stay hydrated throughout the day every day, especially if you're in a hot climate. Bring a glass or BPA free plastic water bottle with you that you can refill as you go. Of course, make sure the water in your destination is safe to drink before you do this. Otherwise, you should buy bottled water in your destination, preferably in a big bottle (so you create less plastic landfill waste) that you can decant into your reusable water bottle.

Alcohol packs a lot of calories and little nutrition, so skip the sugary cocktails. But if you're in Italy or France, you might want to indulge in some wine while you're there. You can check what's vegan-friendly on Barnivore.com.

Exercise on the road

The good news is that travel often involves a lot of walking, whether that's around museums, shopping districts or historical areas. When possible, opt for walking tours (they're often free in European cities!) to see the sights rather than bus or river boat tours. Or download an audio walking tour to your phone. Consider downloading an app to track your fitness. There are plenty of free apps to track your walking, and some phones even come with this functionality built in (as do smart watches). They'll show you how many steps and how many miles you walked, plus how many calories you burned.

Start your day with exercise. Although you will likely be doing plenty of walking, it's always a good idea to start your day with exercise. Many hotels have gyms or pools; if yours doesn't, try going for a run or walk nearby, or jogging up and down the hotel stairs.

If your hotel doesn't have a gym, look for one nearby. Some gyms allow short-term memberships or day passes. (A number of gyms even offer free one-day trials, but shhh, don't tell anyone I told you that!) Or look for fitness classes, which usually allow drop-ins at a drop-in rate. For example, you might be able to find a yoga class or tai chi in the park for a one-time, drop-in rate of $10. Plus, you'll get to meet some locals!

Unfortunately, unless you're prepared to carry a lot of extra weight in your luggage (or pay overweight baggage fees to your airline) you can't bring your weights with you. However, if you go on Youtube, you can find a lot of free videos showing resistance routines. These use your own body weight instead of weights to build muscle mass. You can also lift tin cans or hotel lamps (after you remove the lightbulbs!).

Packing & Safety

If you take vitamins, bring them with you. If you want to make sure you're getting optimum nutrition, even hundreds of miles away from your blender and dehydrator, a superfood mix is an easy way to make sure you're still getting greens and nutrients in your diet, even on the road. This superfood blend (just mix with water) is gluten-free, GMO-free, vegan and sugar-free: http://amzn.to/2kWeQ9P

If you experience nausea, skip the meds and try out nausea bands, which are a more natural technique. They use acupressure to stimulate a pressure point on your wrist and alleviate travel sickness: http://amzn.to/2jDLmfv

Probiotics are also a healthy travel essential, especially if you suffer from not being quite so "regular" when you travel. (A common ailment when flying, as air travel tends to dehydrate as well as wreak havoc on your digestive system!) Good sources of vegan probiotics include kombucha, live-cultured vegan yogurt, fermented vegetables (like sauerkraut or kimchi) and fermented soy products such as tempeh. It's of course always best to get your probiotics through natural food sources, but if you can't then vegan capsules like these ones from Deva are a good alternative: http://amzn.to/2jVPGb8

Resistance bands are cheap, lightweight and easy to pack, and can make your workouts much more satisfying. Pick some up at your local sporting goods store or a kit like this on Amazon: http://amzn.to/2khzX7a

SteriPens are devices that use ultraviolet light to purify water, killing up to 99% of bacteria. It can sterilize up to half a liter of water in under a minute: http://amzn.to/2jVM7BX

If you're going abroad, check whether you need any vaccinations or medications such as anti-malarials before you go. This information is available on the State Department's website, or check with your doctor: http://bit.ly/2kRNGou
UK citizens should check the government's foreign travel advice website:

http://bit.ly/2kWa642

Lastly, do your ears hurt when flying? That's because of pressure changes. Earplugs that vent pressure (not just any old foam earplug!) can help alleviate that pain. You can buy Ear Planes here: http://amzn.to/2kr6k5L

* * *

Section 9:

Emergency Recipes for the Road: Food to Cook Anywhere.

• •

If you are staying somewhere with a kitchen, this last section is for you. Here are a handful of simple recipes you can make in a small or limited kitchen (or in the case of a couple recipes, in an electrical drip brew coffeemaker, the kind common in the US).

Useful Tools to Have With You

- Reusable or disposable bowls and/or plates. Plates can double as chopping boards! Try using the ironing board as a work surface if you don't have a table or desk, or need more space.

- Pocket knife/Swiss army knife for chopping (make sure you pack this in your checked bag, not carry-on!)

- Reusable or disposable cutlery Try these:
  US orders: http://amzn.to/2ksINku
  UK orders: http://amzn.to/2eE8BYk

- Scissors

- Can opener

- Vegetable peeler

- Corkscrew

Useful items in your hotel room:

- Coffeemaker or kettle

- Microwave

——————— Recipes ——————→

Soup in a Coffeemaker

Equipment needed: coffeemaker, bowl and spoon

1. Supermarket: Buy a can of your favorite soup.

2. In hotel: Turn on the coffeemaker. Pour the soup into the glass coffee pot and turn on, but don't fill any water in the water filter (unless you want to water down your soup). The hot plate under the glass coffee pot will heat up your soup.

Salad

Equipment needed: plate, fork and knife

1. Supermarket: Pick up some lettuce and your favorite vegetables, plus a can of beans of your choice. Look for miniature bottles of vinegar and olive oil for the dressing.

2. In hotel: Wash veg in bathroom sink, chop vegetables on the plate with your knife. Arrange on the plate, top with dressing and you're done!

*Please be careful and only do this in countries where the water is safe! In countries where the drinking water is not safe (e.g. India) do NOT buy and consume raw, uncooked vegetables.

Couscous in a coffeemaker

Equipment needed: hotel room coffeemaker or kettle, bowl, plate and fork or spoon.

1. Supermarket: Buy couscous, your favorite vegetables and beans, and a sauce or spice mix if you want.

2. In hotel room: Heat water in the coffeemaker until as close to boiling as possible, then pour over a bowl of couscous. Put the plate on top of the bowl so the couscous cooks for several minutes. You can steam vegetables as well, in an inch or so of water in the glass coffee jar. Put them on the heat until they have steamed through. Add beans and you have a filling meal!

Bean Burritos

Equipment needed: plate, knife, possibly a can opener

1. Supermarket: Buy tortillas, a can of refried beans
    (get one with an easy-open top if possible, or ask at
    hotel reception if they have a can opener you can
    borrow), black olives, tomatoes, salsa, avocado.

2. In hotel room: This one's so simple! Chop up your
    olives and tomatoes and slice your avocado. Put it all
    in the tortilla and roll it up!

Avocado on Toast

Equipment needed: toaster, plate, bowl, knife

1. Supermarket: Buy bread and avocado, and, if you're feeling fancy, a lemon.
2. In hotel room: If you don't have a toaster and are staying in a hotel, check if there's a toaster in the breakfast room they'll let you use. Toast the bread, cut the avocado and mash in the bowl. Put the mashed avocado on the toast and top with a sprinkle of lemon juice.

Oatmeal in a Coffeemaker

Equipment needed: hotel room coffeemaker, bowl, spoon

1. Supermarket: Buy oatmeal (and a bottle of water if you're in a country where tap water shouldn't be consumed).

2. In hotel room: Put the oats and water in the coffeemaker, heat until cooked.

Sandwiches

PB & J, hummus and tomato slices, vegetable pâté, tofu (like the pre-cooked and marinated Taifun variety you can get across Europe) & vegetables

Equipment needed: plate, knife

1. Supermarket: Buy bread or wrap and your favorite fillings.

2. In hotel room: Make the sandwich. (Does this require any more explanation?)

Baked Potato in a Microwave

Equipment needed: microwave, knife, plate, fork

1. Supermarket: Buy potatoes, toppings (I suggest vegetarian baked beans without pork – British-style!).

2. In hotel room: Wash the potato, dry and prick several times with the prongs of a fork. Heat potato in the microwave for 5 minutes. Turn over and cook for another 4-5 minutes until soft. Remove, slice open and add toppings and return for another 1-2 minutes until the toppings are heated.

One-pot Pasta

Equipment needed: one pot, knife, plate or chopping board, plate to eat, fork

Best done in a hostel or holiday apartment kitchen.

1. Supermarket: Buy olive oil, 8oz pasta in your favorite shape, 1½ cups of vegetable stock or water, cherry tomatoes, garlic, onion, basil, vegetables of your choice.

2. In your hotel or apartment kitchen: Chop up the garlic, tomatoes and vegetables.

3. Add the oil to your pot and heat over medium heat. Add the garlic and onion and sauté until just browned.

4. Add the tomatoes, stock/water and pasta and bring to a boil. Stir to submerge the pasta.

5. Reduce the heat to medium-low and cover, adding the other vegetables according to how long it will take them to cook through. You need to cook the pasta for around 7-9 minutes or until the pasta is al dente (look at the instructions on the package). Sprinkle basil on top and serve.

Chili

Equipment needed: microwave, bowl, can opener, plate, knife

1. Supermarket: Buy a can of kidney beans, pinto beans or other beans as desired, onion, garlic, can of chopped tomatoes, chilli powder and cumin powder

2. In hotel room: Chop onion and garlic and add to the bowl. Add the rest of the ingredients to the bowl and microwave for 5 minutes. Stir and microwave another 3-4 minutes.

Snack: Hummus with Dip-able Items

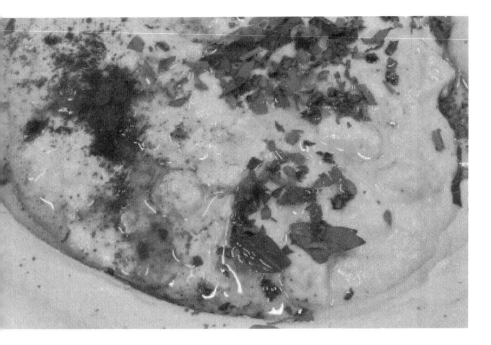

Equipment needed: None

Buy a tub of hummus, a loaf of crusty French bread, crackers, vegetable sticks, or cherry tomatoes. Dip and enjoy – simple!

*Check the hummus ingredients – in some places (France, for example), they add dairy products or creme fraiche to hummus!

Snack: Trail mix

Equipment needed: Bowl or a plastic bag

Buy a mix of different nuts, seeds and dried fruits (plus some dark chocolate or cacao nibs if you want a treat) and mix up in a plastic bag. This is best done by buying small portions of each from a bulk bin.

Instant Food

Buy some of these from Trader Joe's and heat in the microwave or by submerging the packet in hot water from the coffeemaker or kettle: http://amzn.to/1XlozCd.

Tips

A few final tips on emergency cooking. If you're staying somewhere where the water is safe to drink (and wash your vegetables in), you can create your own salad spinner with a resealable (Ziploc) bag. Put your salad greens in a resealable bag and fill with water. Then, poke holes in the bag and hang it up with a clothespin while the excess water drains from the holes. Shake a few times until all the water drains out. To keep items cool without a fridge, fill an ice bucket with ice and place items in it, or in cold climates, place items outside on a balcony.

Design your meals to contain each of the following: grains, vegetables and proteins. Grains can include: instant ramen, oatmeal, couscous, bread or quick-cooking rice noodles (the thin kind often sold in the Asian section of the supermarket, which you can rehydrate in boiled water in 3-5 minutes). Choose hearty vegetables and fruit and that don't require refrigeration or cooking, like bananas, apples, oranges, dried fruits, tomatoes, onions, carrots, cucumbers and bell peppers. Look for proteins that don't need to be cooked, such as nuts (walnuts, almonds, cashews), seeds (sunflower seeds, pumpkin seeds), vacuum packed (UHT) tofu, peanut butter or canned beans. Then, dress up your meals using spices, oil, vinegar, soy sauce and salt and peppers, or other condiments that don't need to be refrigerated.

Finally, if you can't pack a Swiss Army knife (like if you're traveling with a carry-on only), buy an inexpensive paring knife to prepare your meals and leave it behind in your hotel.

* * *

Section 10:

Final Tips & Resources.

Before I send you off on your merry way, here are a few final tips and resources, from the top vegan restaurants of 2017 to the best vegan travel destinations this year, plus what to do after your trip. Plus, a gift to you for reading this book!

After Your Trip

By now, you've hopefully had an excellent trip filled with delicious vegan food. Once you're home, don't forget to share your experiences with others! Help out future vegan travelers by leaving reviews on TripAdvisor, HappyCow or Foursquare.

I'd love to hear from you. If you discover a great vegan restaurant, tell me about it at **hello@theveganword.com**.

If you have a blog, inspire and assist other vegans by writing up a post about your trip, including information about the restaurants you visited, what vegan dishes appear on the menu, and how you rate the food.

If you used information from any blogs, or got information from people on social media, thank them! You might think that they're too busy to care about your messages, but everyone likes to be thanked. They've put in the effort of putting together blog posts or information for you, so let them know it helped you.

Did you discover a restaurant had closed? Let the blogger know, and report it to HappyCow and TripAdvisor.

Last, tell others (vegan and non-vegans alike) about your experiences, and dispel the myth that vegan travel is difficult and boring and involves long slogs through the streets looking for food, or eating nothing but canned chickpeas!

Resources & Recommendations

Get this list online: theveganword.com/travel-resources

The Vegan Word
theveganword.com

HappyCow
happycow.net

VegGuide
vegguide.org

VegDining
vegdining.com

HappyCow App
iOS ($3.99): bit.ly/happycowitunes
Android ($3.99): bit.ly/happycowapp

VeganXpress App
iOS ($1.99): bit.ly/veganxpress

Vegman App
iOS (free): bit.ly/vegmanapp

North American Vegetarian Society (NAVS)
navs-online.org

Couchsurfing

couchsurfing.com

Meetup
meetup.com

Post Punk Kitchen Forums
forum.theppk.com

Vegan Forum
veganforum.org

iBarnivore
iOS (free): bit.ly/ibarnivore

Vegaholic
iOS ($1.99): bit.ly/vegaholic

VegeTipple
Android ($1.49): bit.ly/vegetipple

Evernote
evernote.com

Pocket
getpocket.com

Doodle
doodle.com

European Vegan Zine

bit.ly/euveganzine

Vegan Passport
bit.ly/veganpassport4

Hotels.com
hotels.com

Lastminute
lastminute.com

Hotel Tonight (App)
iOS (free): bit.ly/hoteltonightitunes
Android (free): bit.ly/hoteltonightandroid

Hostel World
hostelworld.com

Hostel Bookers
hostelbookers.com

Airbnb (please note this is a referral, so if you sign up and use the service you will receive $37 in credit, and so will I)
airbnb.co.uk/c/caitling58?s=8

Vegvisits
vegvisits.com

TrustedHousesitters
www.trustedhousesitters.com

Tripadvisor

tripadvisor.com

Homeaway

homeaway.com

Lush

lush.com

Wikitravel

wikitravel.org

Is it Vegan? (App) – you can scan a barcode and it will tell you if the product is vegan (best results in the US)
iOS ($4.99): bit.ly/isitveganapp / Android: bit.ly/isitveganandroid

Vegan Travel Club (this is an affiliate link, so if you sign up using it I'll get a small fee, at no extra cost to you)
https://vegantravelclub.com/?ref=19

Refillable, BPA-free toothpaste tubes

http://amzn.to/2jSta5n

Airline carry-on sized Jason natural toothpaste:

US orders: http://amzn.to/2kRKFQP
UK orders: http://amzn.to/2kNN7Zx

Jason Mineral Sunblock

http://amzn.to/2kRPIkf

Kiss My Face Sun Spray

http://amzn.to/2kp1u95

Jason Kids Sunscreen

http://amzn.to/2kRV8vD

Green People Organic Sun Lotion

http://amzn.to/2kP7g4L

Green People Children's Scent Free Sun Lotion

http://amzn.to/2kP3lER

Hurraw! SPF lip balm

http://amzn.to/2kRO6He

Lavera After Sun

http://amzn.to/2kRZeUw

Green People After Sun

http://amzn.to/2kRKrJq

Beat-It All Natural DEET-Free Spray

http://amzn.to/2jSESgf

Jason Quit Bugging Me Spray

http://amzn.to/2kRSgiD

Incognito Spray

http://amzn.to/2kOX5gG

Jason's Tea Tree deodorant

http://amzn.to/2koMR5p

Lavanila deodorant

http://amzn.to/2jst0TH

Fit Pit

http://thegreenwoman.co.uk

Vitamin A Swimwear

https://vitaminaswim.com

Powdered soymilk

US orders: http://amzn.to/2jSrQwY

UK orders: http://amzn.to/2ko9Cqq

Koyo instant ramen

http://amzn.to/2kRT9rd

Vegan Camp

vegancamp.co.uk

Vegan Cruise

vegancruises.eu

Raw Vegan Cruise

http://bit.ly/2jYgLwE

Vegan River Cruises

veganrivercruises.com

Vegan Options in Chain Restaurants (US)

http://bit.ly/2ksgwuB

Vegan Options in Chain Restaurants (UK)

http://bit.ly/2ksmRpZ

The Farm Retreat

thefarmatsanbenito.com

Olive Retreat

oliveretreat.com

Yoga Detox Retreats

yogadetoxretreats.co.uk

Veg Voyages

vegvoyages.com

Teen VGN Summer Camp (UK)

teenvgn.com/camp

Vegan Camp (California, USA)

vegancamp.org

Vegan Surf Camp

uk.vegansurfcamp.com

Bring Fido

bringfido.com

Doggity (Free, iOS)

http://apple.co/2kSGoh7

Pet Travel

pettravel.com

Superfood Blend (mix with water)

http://amzn.to/2kWeQ9P

Travel Sickness/Anti Nausea Acupressure Bands

http://amzn.to/2jDLmfv

Deva Probiotic Capusules

http://amzn.to/2jVPGb8

Resistance Band Kit

http://amzn.to/2khzX7a

SteriPen

http://amzn.to/2jVM7BX

US State Department (for foreign travel advice)

http://bit.ly/2kRNGou

UK Government Foreign Travel Advice

http://bit.ly/2kWa642

EarPlanes

http://amzn.to/2kr6k5L

Travel cutlery

http://amzn.to/2ksINku

Top Vegan Restaurants Worldwide

(Source, HappyCow.net rankings, as of January 2017)

1. The Wala Room – Torremolinos, Spain
2. The Vegan Nom Food Truck – Austin, Texas, USA
3. The Veggie Grill – San Jose, California, USA
4. Just 4 U Vegan Kitchen and Market – Tampa, Florida, USA
5. Super Jami – Stuttgart, Germany
6. Cuenco – Mendoza, Argentina
7. Krawummel – Munester, Germany
8. Virtuous Pie – Vancouver, British Columbia, Canada
9. Crazy Bean Cafe – Great Bookham, UK
10. The V Factor – Lanzarote, Canary Islands, Spain

With thanks to HappyCow.net for allowing us to use this data. Accurate as of January 2017.

Top Vegan Destinations of 2017

Los Angeles, California, USA

Los Angeles has the largest number of vegan restaurants on the West Coast of the US, and its variety blows away visitors. At *Crossroads*, you can taste vegan fine dining from chef Tal Ronnen, who has been featured on Oprah. At *Plant Food + Wine*, taste creations from chef Matthew Kenney, who won two prestigious James Beard nominations for Rising Star and who was named *Food and Wine* magazine's Best New Chef in 1994. At *Plant Food + Wine*, you can expect to sample delights such as vegan blue cheese with shaved fennel, kumquat marmalade and grilled Lodge bread or butternut - potato gnocchi with farro bolognese.

Berlin, Germany

Berlin is fast becoming known as one of the best cities in the world for vegans. With 26 fully vegan restaurants and counting, Berlin has something that will suit all tastes – from raw and healthy *Café Laauma* to vegan creperie *Let it Be*. Berlin is also home to "vegan street" (*Schivelbeinerstrasse*), a block-long stretch in Prenzlauerberg which hosts *Avesu*, a vegan shoe shop, *Dear Goods*, a vegan clothing and bag store, *Veganz*, a vegan supermarket and the attached *Goodies Café*.

Taipei, Taiwan

Taipei might not be the first city that springs to mind when considering vegan destinations, but with some reports stating that forty percent of the population practices vegetarianism at least part of the time (mainly for religious reasons, following Buddhist practices), it's very vegetarian- and vegan-friendly. Vegetarian restaurants grace nearly every block, so you're never far from veggie food. Buffet restaurants are popular, and for breakfast you can pick up fresh-cut tropical fruit from a market or a fruit stall on the street. Beware that mock meats may contain egg or milk extract, so best to steer clear of those and stick with well-known dishes (like vegetable or tofu) unless you can confirm the absence of animal products. Food in Taipei is also inexpensive compared to the U.S. or Western Europe, and you can dine in high-class style at *Yu Shan Ge* (popular with Taiwanese celebrities) and eat a 9-course meal for around $30.

Rome, Italy

Pasta lovers rejoice! Italy's turning increasingly vegan-friendly. In addition to traditional Italian dishes that are often vegan, more and more vegan restaurants are opening. *Arancia Blu* combines fine arts and events with vegan food while *Zazie* is the place to go for healthy and fresh, vegetable-centric meals. Don't forget that a lot of traditional fruit-based gelatos are vegan, not to mention that more and more gelaterias in Italy are offering soy- and rice-based gelatos for their lactose-intolerant customers!

New York City, New York, USA

In New York, you can find just about any cuisine you'd ever want – including a huge selection of vegetarian and vegan food. From a vegan cheese shop, *Dr. Cow Tree Nut Cheese*, to a vegan shoe shop, *Moo Shoes*, New York has it all. Want a vegan coat? *Vaute Couture*, a high-end vegan coat line, is also based in New York. Of course, you can dine on some of the best vegan food in the world at restaurants like *Candle 79*.

Paris, France

Paris might have a reputation for being one of the least vegetarian-friendly cities in the world, but the French capital is changing. From veggie burgers at *Hank's* to healthy vegan fare at *Cafe Ginger*, Paris is becoming more plant-based. For a treat, check out the *Gentle Gourmet* for high-end vegan dining; their vegan lasagna with homemade cashew cheese is extremely popular, and they were one of the first places to make vegan macarons!

Mexico City, Mexico

North America's largest city is undergoing somewhat of a vegan revolution. Vegan street food fans needn't be left out; vegan taco stand *Por Siempre Vegano* offers fresh tortillas and a selection of vegan meats prepared al pastor (crispy, thin shavings of mock meat, shawarma-style) or as chorizo (spicy vegan sausage). *Los Loosers* will deliver vegan food to your door using their bike delivery service.

London, England

England is the birthplace of Donald Watson, The Vegan Society and the vegan movement, so naturally London is host to a large vegan scene. London has a thriving vegan scene from old favourites like *Manna* (London's oldest vegetarian restaurant, now turned vegan) to *Mildred's* (an extremely popular and busy vegetarian restaurant in Soho, now with branches in Camden and King's Cross), to newcomers like *Kabaret @ Karamel*, a vegan bar. London also boasts the largest vegan social group in the world, the *London Vegan Meetup* [www.meetup.com/londonvegan/], which has vegan events nearly every day.

Singapore

This diverse city-state was chosen as the second most vegan-friendly city in Asia in 2016 by PETA Asia. At *Lotus Vegetarian*, you can get Taiwanese-style vegetarian dishes, while *VeganBurg* offers up a big selection of vegan burgers. *Miao Yi* is perfect if you're craving vegan Chinese food, or head to *Whole Earth Vegetarian* for Thai-style food.

Barcelona, Spain

Barcelona's vegan scene is growing quickly and surprising many in a land that worships chorizo and jamon (ham, which is liberally put on just about every dish in Spain). In addition to old favorites like upscale restaurant *Teresa Carles*, Barcelona's burgeoning vegan scene now counts a vegetarian and vegan pizzeria, *Dolce Pizza y los Veganos*, a vegan and mostly gluten-free bakery, *Pastisseria La Besneta*, a vegan shoe shop, *Amapola*, and three vegan grocery stores. Plus there's a growing number of raw and healthy eateries and shops like *Eattitude, Petit Brot, Vacka* and *The Living Food*. Not to mention the fact that in 2016 Barcelona declared itself a Veg-Friendly City!

Toronto, Canada

Satisfy your junk food cravings with vegan chicken waffles at *Hogtown Vegan* or vegan pizza and doughnuts at *Apiecalypse Now*! Or if you're looking for healthier fare, check out *Rawlicious*, which serves healthy, organic and raw vegan dishes, such as pad thai made with zucchini and kelp noodles.

* * *

Your Free Gift

As a thank you for buying this book, I've made you a free gift! It's a wallet-sized translation card to carry abroad. You can show it to waiters around the world to ask for vegan food, even if you don't speak the local language.

Claim your free gift here: https://theveganword.com/evtg-gift

Once you enter your email address, you'll be sent the wallet card by email.

Bonus! Get 20% off your first *Vegan Trip Planner* service. Feeling like DIY isn't for Y-O-U? While the Essential Vegan Travel Guide shows you how to plan your perfect vegan trip the DIY way, if you're too time-crunched to look up veganrestaurants, sit back and let us do the work for you.

The *Vegan Trip Planner* service is perfect if you don't have time to implement all the strategies in this guidebook. Tell us your destination and requirements (gluten-free, raw, etc.) and we'll write you a personalized vegan itinerary. Order yours here with the discount code "evtgfr" to get 20% off: https://theveganword.com/trip-planner/

Thank you!

Thank you so much for reading this! Please tell me about your favorite vegan-friendly city in the world so that it can be considered for next year's Top Vegan Destinations. Email me at hello@theveganword.com.

If you enjoyed it, please tell your vegetarian or vegan friends and family about it. I'd also like to ask you to share a review on Amazon – because of the Amazon algorithm, the more reviews that appear on Amazon, the more Amazon recommends this book to customers. This, in turn, will help keep this guidebook on the Amazon bestseller list. And the more Amazon recommends the book, the more people can take stress-free, totally vegan vacations (and not resort to eating chickpeas from a can, or worse – give up being vegan on the road because they think it's not feasible!).

Acknowledgments

I'd like to thank everyone who helped me with this book, for giving up their evenings and weekends and free time to help me. I'd especially like to thank Deloris of Prodesigns (https://www.fiverr.com/prodesignsx) for the gorgeous cover design, and Loki Lillistone, for the beautiful layout design. I also want to extend a huge thanks to my team of readers for their invaluable feedback and advice:

Alison Classe

Gillian Pollock (Guid Publications)

Cadry Nelson (cadryskitchen.com)

Rika (veganmiam.com)

Joey (flickingthevs.blogspot.com)

Nikki Scott (South East Asia Backpacker, South America Backpacker and Europe Backpacker)

Tom Galer-Unti

Regina Galer-Unti

And last, I'd like to thank my puppy, Benito, for reminding me when it was time to stop writing and take him for a walk outside in the sun.

The Vegan Word Travel Guidebooks...

Check out the whole series of current and upcoming guidebooks:
https://theveganword.com/guidebooks/